Esca

Escape
to reality

Tony Ralls
with
David B. Hall

New Wine Press

First published 1985. New Wine Press edition 1988

New Wine Press,
P.O. Box 17,
Chichester PO20 6RY,
England

ISBN 0 947852 43 3

Printed and bound in Great Britain by
Hazell Watson & Viney Limited
Member of BPCC plc
Aylesbury, Bucks, England

Contents

This book is dedicated to the many who need to hear there is hope, to the many reaching out in Jesus name in very difficult situations, and especially to those who both past and present have been used by Jesus to support me, without whom I would never have made it.

Tony Ralls

The author of this book may be contacted at:

The YMCA,
Mill Street,
Sidmouth,
Devon.

Forword

I first met Tony in 1978. I was looking for Christians, involved in prisons, to invite to a meeting in Church House, Westminster, to which we had invited Chuck Colson to tell us about Prison Fellowship in the United States. We wanted to see if we could start Prison Fellowship in Britain. Friends of mine told me to invite Tony, a remarkable young man, an ex-prisoner and ex-drug addict himself who had become a new person through becoming a Christian, and had a growing ministry to prisoners.

That first big meeting in Church House ended in apparent disaster. I went home deeply depressed feeling I had failed the Lord and that Prison Fellowship hadn't started. Tuesday I was at my lowest, I received a lovely letter from Tony. Amongst other things he said: "God wants to encourage you because you have just given birth to a spiritual baby, and you are suffering from post-natal depression. And it doesn't matter about being weak and foolish, because God uses weak things and foolish things."

Since that time I have received many letters from Tony, and always amazingly, he has put his finger on the place where I was spiritually at the time in my thoughts about Prison Fellowship.

Tony has been a member of our staff team for a number of years, and for the last couple of years as the South West Regional Co-ordinator. In the last two years he has toured with his Life Presentation team during Prisoners Week, – a team consisting of ex-prisoners and ex-drug addicts, and it has been so moving and encouraging to hear how their lives have been changed through Christ.

I feel very honoured indeed to have been invited to write a foreword for this book. I believe Tony, and his lovely wife Linda have a most remarkable ministry. They are a trophy of God's grace. And I pray that many prisoners will find inspiration from these pages to join the army of "weak and foolish things" that God picks up to confound the wise and mighty with, and that many others will be encouraged to obey Christ's commission to his church: "When I was in prison you came to me."

Sylvia Mary Alison

1: Last chance

It had been a long, long night. Tossing and turning on the bed of my cell in Pentonville Prison didn't just mark the end of a six month sentence; I knew it was my final opportunity to shrug off the life-style that had been close to killing me.

I looked at my own clothes – returned the previous night to replace the prison uniform I had worn for so long. Lying across the chair alongside the bed were a pair of tatty, faded, jeans, a crumpled, stained T-shirt, a jacket that a tramp might reject (though they had all been cleaned) and a pair of boots making up my wardrobe. The boots were the only items of any quality – leather, high-backed, but short on polish.

What a legacy from almost 25 years of living. I fingered two crumpled letters that marked the only fresh aspect of my life. One was from a girl I had met months before, telling me about a Christian community which she claimed could help me shake off the drug habit. The other was from that same community – inviting me to spend some time with them.

Somehow I knew it was a last chance. If I couldn't soon break free of the world of drugs I knew I wouldn't last much longer. And after spending more of the last ten years inside penal establishments than outside I knew that this was a dead-end also.

I cheered myself with a thought: once out of this place I was going to have one last fling, one final fix!

The prison was silent, a thousand or so men were yet to be roused. I sensed the approach of the prison officer even before the key sounded in the lock. I clambered down from my bunk. Dressing took a few seconds and I followed after him on to the landing. 'Look at the scruff,' came a chuckle from the opposite landing – it was one of the other prisoners being released with me. Had he been nearer I think I would have risked losing the remission I had earned. He stood smug and smart in a flashy, stylish suit; his blond hair slicked back. For four months he had respected me as a tough, prison-hardened mate. Now he saw me for what I was beginning to realise myself to be – grubby, broken, useless.

He called again: 'Didn't know you were a junkie.' I hadn't realised my appearance revealed my addiction so readily. I tried to keep up a good front, pursing my lips and slouching along.

Breakfast should have been an exciting affair; I was, after all, only minutes from freedom. Instead the congealed mess seemed to stick to the plate. 'Eat your porridge and you won't be back,' was the screw's favourite phrase . . . he didn't have to face the porridge.

The discharge routine slowly rumbled along . . . now it was the summary return of my personal property. Not much . . . one wrinkled diary plopped from the official brown paper envelope on to the counter. With it fell my charge sheet and details of the offence for which I was ending the punishment.

My release grant of just over £4 was the only thing that stirred me. As soon as the notes touched my hand I began to calculate the amount of drugs it would buy: four months inside wouldn't have jacked up the price too high.

Seconds later I was free. The small door inside the two massive gates swung open, I stepped out, and the smell of freedom hit me. I hurried to the nearest underground and pushed a pound note through the glass partition muttering 'Piccadilly' as I did so.

The next few minutes were a blur as I prayed that my luck wouldn't fail me in the old haunt. It didn't.

All the time I had a faint stirring of hope that I wouldn't see the prison again, that I was about to take my last dose. But addicts don't count on that too much. Like a sliver of metal flashing towards a magnet I found myself drawn inexorably on, to the top of the escalator . . . I shoved the ticket at the ticket collector and twisted along the circular passage searching. My eyes spotted a familiar face. 'Got any gear?' I asked. With an arch of his eyebrows the face indicated I would find what I wanted at the top of the stairs. With the crowd bustling round me I stumbled to the telephone booths squatting alongside the road. Eros seemed to be pointing his arrow at my back but I wasn't interested. The man I wanted was there. I didn't need to speak – he knew my need and the deal was completed. Just feeling the little glass ampoules of Methadone in my hand seemed to send my head spinning. Perspiration soaked my palms and my heart thumped. First, however, I needed a syringe. I went to the chemists on the edge of the Circus, all the time clutching the glass phials in my pocket. Now I was in business.

I stumbled back down the underground stairs and edged into the gents' toilets. I swore! Every cubicle bore the loathsome signal, engaged; people sleeping before being kicked out by the attendant. The familiar smell of dirty bodies and urine filled my nostrils.

But I couldn't wait, the tension was too great. An attendant was idly pushing a mop along the floor. 'I'm a registered addict – can I use your room?' I gasped. He believed me – or just didn't care – and led me to a broom cupboard where I squeezed among the mops and pans, took a deep breath, and began the operation which no amount of time inside prison could erase from my memory.

First I slipped off my leather belt and wrapped it tightly round my left arm. Then I took one of the glass ampoules. Carefully I snapped off the top putting the tiny fragments on the edge of the mop bucket. The liquid shone in the beam of light through the door as I touched the tip of the needle inside the glass container. Like a surgeon at his gentlest, I carefully eased back the handle, watching the synthetic heroin fill the syringe. I wiped the tip of the needle round the container and repeated the manoeuvre in the minute glass end. Nothing could be missed, each globule of liquid was precious. On television the doctors squirt the needle into the air but I'd learnt not to waste any of the valuable Methadone in that kind of demonstration, so I pressed the handle until the liquid blobbed to the top, bubble-free, and then paused.

I meticulously flicked the syringe to release all the air-bubbles. The ritual was almost completed. With my free hand I twisted the belt tighter to halt the flow of blood in my arm and bring up the vein; as the target swelled I pressed in the needle. There was a slight stab of familiar pain and blood tinged the liquid in the syringe. I squeezed the syringe and watched the liquid disappear from its see-through casing. Almost immediately a feeling of sickness came over me to be instantly swallowed up in a deeper, fuller surge of well-being as my head began to swim.

I nodded, like a plastic dog on the rear windowsill of a car, my inside singing a song that had been silent for months. This was heaven. Still woozy I undid the belt and managed to slip it back round my waist without bothering to slither it through the loops on my trousers. Pulling my jacket on over my shoulders I stumbled out of the cupboard, up the steps and into the crowd, walking with a spring in my step, the morning looking much brighter now. I wasn't going to miss the appointment for my second breakfast of the day, this time at the crypt of St Martin-in-the-Fields Church alongside Trafalgar Square and I knew that I would soon be heading for the Life for the World centre that had offered me the chance at a new future. I also remembered my vow when the men who ran it had visited me in Pentonville: 'You might get me off drugs,' I laughed, 'but you'll never make me a Christian.'

2: The Beginning

I am so happy to say that I have let Jesus Christ come into my life. I would never have thought that someone as bad as I was would – but I did. I am so happy. Before I would not have let him do that. All I have ever done is turn my back on him and all the time Jesus wanted to help me. I do wish I had done it many years ago.

J. Exeter Prison

Some people say the seeds of our behaviour are sown in the first few years of our lives. If that is so I must have been sprinkled liberally early on with seeds that were later to flower defiance and deceit.

I was born Albert John Dansie in Looe, Cornwall, the illegitimate child of a waitress from Plymouth. My mother's stepfather wanted nothing to do with this addition to the household, so I was fostered by another couple living in the same house.

Although my mother paid what she could for my keep the childless foster parents began to exert pressure on her to allow them full control of me. Finally they threatened my mother: 'You either let us adopt the child or you get him back.' With no better prospects of her own she agreed. I was sixteen months old when the switch was recorded officially.

My new father had been discharged from the Pioneer Corps the year before the adoption. We lived in Plymouth and Totnes for a time before the next major change in my life when my father became a farm labourer. My adopted parents lived rent-free in the farm cottage – two living rooms and a scullery downstairs and four rooms upstairs. But after a fall from a ladder father injured his leg and was unable to work.

I was five and attending the local Ivybridge school when a

lodger arrived, one of the only ways my parents could earn money. With most of the furniture having been sold for food the newcomer took the bed in my small room while I slept on a camp bed with a few bedclothes.

Inside a month the lodger had discovered my background, traced my mother to the hotel in which she was now working in Teignmouth, and begun telephoning her. It was because of his persuasion that my mother met me and my foster mother outside Ivybridge Railway Station one afternoon. It was a meeting which time has fortunately cleared from my memory. I looked grubby and unkempt and my mother insisted on taking me back. She took me to her mother in Plymouth and from there I was taken by the National Society for the Prevention of Cruelty to Children – a pawn in an adult game of ownership.

Soon I was moved again – this time to St Vincents, a Roman Catholic Orphanage in Torquay, run by nuns. My memories are vague and disjointed: check-shirts, vast dormitories, and frequent church services. The nuns were quiet but firm. I recall the bonfire night when I was forced to stand outside with my back to the erupting colours as the penalty for having relieved myself in the chapel! I also remember the huge open-air tea-parties with long trestle tables covered with white tablecloths; I enjoyed the sunshine, jelly and buns. In fact it was at one of these parties that I first met the couple who were to become my next set of parents.

I had been told that I might soon have a Mummy and Daddy and was very proud, telling anyone who would listen. Before things were finalised they took me to stay with them for a while and I recall the long journey to South Molton, North Devon. I punctuated the car ride with a hundred questions, usually the same words: 'Are we there yet?'

Soon the move was final and I became Michael Bernard Ralls, adopted son of Mr Ralls, a grocer, and his wife, a health visitor, and brother of John, two and a half years older than myself.

The adoption ceremony was a strange event. I stood for the first time in a court and saw an old man and remembered he had often visited me at the orphanage and given me a silver coin. It was, however, merely another seemingly disjointed event in a life of confusion.

School was exciting, though, and as I settled down I moved from twenty-fifth place in the class to always being in the top ten.

With some doubt about whether the ceremony had been performed when I was a baby it was decided I should be baptised, 'just to be on the safe side,' my new mother said. I didn't understand why I needed salt on my tongue or what they meant when they told me I was completely pure, and I guess it wasn't long before the rest of the congregation began to question that latter part.

As one of the Graveyard gang I was the star performer in our stone-throwing fights and the regular forays around the churchyard when we swung our football boots by their laces as weapons.

It was there that I had my first brush with the police. For throwing a thermos flask under the wheels of a lorry I earned a police visit and a spanking from my parents.

Life at South Molton was pleasant but didn't last long. When my parents moved to Ottery St Mary in East Devon I couldn't adapt to the change. From the local primary school I was sent with my brother John to Winslade Park, a private grammar school run by Marist priests, seven miles away. Although it was a boarding school we lived at home, cycling to and from home each day through the narrow country lanes.

I was also made to visit the local Roman Catholic Church and it was there that I first met the boy who was to become a close friend, Billy Donoghue. Billy and I served mass together. It was here I began to put together the threads of a craft which was to cost me dear in the years to come – stealing. As I bowed before the altar I scooped some of the coins from the collection into my hand, an act I couldn't consider wrong. My only worry was that one day I might get found out.

The years passed quickly. I did moderately well at school, played rugby, studied Latin, and learned to smoke my first cigarette. I was cycling at the time and almost fell off through dizziness. From then on I smoked regularly as often as funds allowed. Because my father was a delivery driver for a grocer's my nicotine stocks were occasionally supplemented by a packet of ten which would go missing from his van.

One Monday I took my dinner money and spent it at the cinema in Exeter instead of going to school. There was no way I could get away with it, but as I learnt to do in later years, I took my punishment and made a personal resolution not to get caught next time.

With my fifteenth birthday on the horizon I decided to join the Army. My parents took some persuading but finally agreed and I passed the examination for the Royal Army Service Corps. Soon after my birthday I stood in the recruiting office, held up my hand and took the oath. The next nine years of my life were to be given to Queen and Country. Except that it didn't quite work out that way.

3. Soldier's life

I will be 37 in August. This in my first prison sentence – I am doing four years, but I have been in trouble before. My wife is now seeking a divorce and that's breaking my heart as this would be our sixth anniversary. I have taken Jesus as my saviour and trust in him with all my heart.

T. Wakefield Prison

The train rumbled on towards its destination, Hobbs Platoon Quebec Barracks, Bordon, near Aldershot. I was uncertain what to expect but felt the simmerings of excitement. As the journey continued more and more men in uniform joined the train, including a sprinkling of nervous faces looking very anxious like myself.

'All for Bordon Camp to the lorry outside the station,' stammered the tannoy as the train rumbled to a halt. I plunged into the milling throng assembling alongside the billowing canvas of the army vehicle. The sergeant's booming voice instructed us to climb in with our gear when our names were called. 'Our Queen and Country depend on you – heaven help us. But I will make soldiers of you. The army will make or break you,' he threatened, and followed it with the list of names. The gaggle of recruits replied, some with the correct 'Yes sergeant,' others with 'yessir,' 'present' and even ''ere I am mate.' A vague flicker in the corner of the sergeant's mouth promised plenty, even though he didn't respond.

One after the other we ran to the back of the lorry, grabbing a short rope and pulling ourselves up . . . one took a jump over the tail-gate and a couple raised a titter when they toppled off. As the lorry jerked into life we sat round the sides staring at each other. It was a tense, awkward silence, occasionally broken by a muttered comment from one of the sixteen figures which attracted the attention of the other fifteen pairs of eyes.

Eventually a white pole barred the lorry's way. 'Another bunch of glory boys?' chuckled a corporal, standing alongside what I later discovered was the guardhouse.

Polished brass and white paintwork was my first view of the guardhouse . . . I was to see it from a different angle in the not-too-distant future. We jerked forward again and oblong red-brick buildings flashed by the back of the lorry, each connected by a series of steps and concrete paths. Every so often a group of soldiers marched past, arms swinging, heads erect and heels cracking in unison.

Within seconds of the lorry screeching to a halt the sergeant's face appeared at the back. 'All out,' he ordered and as the tail-gate crashed down we stumbled out to form a line – tallest to the shortest. That sounded simple enough but we fumbled around before the final order was achieved.

'Listen you lot,' barked the sergeant who had been joined by a corporal. 'This is your corporal. He has the dubious privilege of living with you. You will find where his room is and go there if you need anything.'

It was now that the whole adventure began to take on a more serious nature. The sergeant, face red and voice gradually toughening, began to lay the groundwork for the discipline which was to follow.

'I am a sergeant and will be called "sergeant." I am not a mate – if I wanted a mate I wouldn't choose one of you lot. I am not a sir – much as I am honoured by your respect, I was never dubbed a knight. If you want to know anything, you come to attention and say "Permission to speak, sergeant".'

His voice thundered on. We had twenty-four hours to decide whether we wanted to stay in the army, after that it was a case of buying ourselves out. We were each to be paid two pounds fifteen shillings a week – one pound and five shillings of it to be banked for us.

Lecture over, we surged down the steps to the barracks led by the corporal with his clip-board. Through the door was a staircase and next to it the corporal's room, his name on a dull, painted plaque decorating the door. On the right was the washroom with sinks and toilets and the smell of disinfectant and next to that a dormitory of about twenty beds. Steel lockers, backing on to each other between each bed, provided a measure of privacy. The floor was polished wood and a pot-bellied stove glowed red and welcoming in the centre of the room. Some recruits, early arrivals, were already busy; a couple were ironing their clothes, one was running a hot iron over his boot toe-caps to get the pimples off and others were using soft-cloths to rub their boots and the chinstraps of their hats. They kept up a constant circular motion, pausing only occasionally to dab the cloth into the polish or to spit on it. Naively I asked one what he was doing. 'Bulling my boots, mate,' he replied. I was to learn that trick and find it was second nature before long.

The corporal began to rattle off names and numbers. I was 23730597 Ralls, private; a title that was to become as easy to say as my name. With three names already behind me what was a new one, even if it did take a numerical form?

I suddenly found myself staring at the heads of the early arrivals. They all looked the same: short hair, and from an inch above their ears down they had the appearance of plucked chickens.

'Put a pudding basin on you and just shear round,' a Londoner chortled, observing my stare. One newcomer gasped. The Londoner turned to him: 'Yours will be worse – it's too long.' The long-haired lad looked thoughtful. When we next looked he had gone. We never did see him again.

'Fall in for food all new arrivals,' shouted the corporal and we fumbled to carry out his instruction, 'Three rows, one pace apart.' After a few seconds of confusion we managed something resembling order.

'Right turn,' brought more chaos as several of us found ourselves face to face with each other. It took time before we managed to get it right, but not without a casualty. One of the lads lifted his leg correctly, stamped his foot down with great determination, only to find his other foot underneath.

Eventually our shambling procession made it to the canteen. metal tray, plate, and a few dollops of what passed for food later we were ready to visit the barber. With astonishing speed he reduced our varied locks to a uniform egg-look.

Next stop was the stores. 'Drawers, cellular, two; shirts, khaki, two . . .' the supply sergeant's voice droned on monotonously. Without asking any measurements he sized each individual up and flicked across a selection of clothing. I staggered back to the barracks with a kit-bag over one shoulder and my arms piled so high I could scarcely see where I was going. I'd hardly dropped the pile on the bed before I was instructed to join the nervous giggling crowd outside the medical room.

'Cough and drop, mate. That's all,' called one fellow through the corner of his mouth as he came out. He was right. My hands slid self-consciously over my crotch. I had never stood naked in front of anyone before. 'Seen one, see 'em all, son,' said the doctor. And hardly having time to check the stethoscope which brushed my chest, he waved me away.

My first six months passed quickly. I enjoyed the newness of it all and after the first shambles of a drill we began to shape up, wheeling and turning as well as any of the groups. I was to be a clerk so typing lessons were added to my routine. After the first few weeks we were allowed out but there was little to do other than a wander into the town or a ride to nearby Aldershot which was about as lively as a seafront on a wet day in November.

But as six months ticked by things started to go wrong. Or rather I started to go wrong.

We were in Cornwall camping for a few days when I ate the solid fuel. It was a simple plan; I was bored and wanted to avoid the next exercise which involved camping on Bodmin Moor with nothing more than a couple of army raincoats for shelter. It was raining, I was wet and had had enough. I reasoned that if I 'accidentally' ate some of the fuel they would send me back to camp. The sergeant peered at me gloomily from the outline of his bivouac. 'What is it?' he asked.

'I woke up and reached for something to eat. It tasted funny so I lit a match and saw it wasn't hardtack but solid fuel.' I let my voice trail away to sound genuinely worried.

Taken to the lieutenant I had another sympathetic hearing. 'Never mind, private,' he said. 'This will help you feel better.' He gave me a tot of whisky and sent me back to the squad.

It was my first attempt at dodging – not a success.

Once back at Bordon, life went on as usual but all too soon it was time for exercises again. My mind worked overtime, searching for the perfect excuse: one that would prevent me from taking part but wouldn't rob me of my imminent leave.

I decided on a cut, taking a single edged razor blade into the washroom to perform the operation. Holding the sharp edge alongside my flesh, however, merely caused my courage to dribble away.

A friend offered to help. Before I could blink he slashed a slick line between forefinger and thumb. There was no pain but blood gushed out with success indicated by each red spurt. I was rushed to the medical officer and ushered into a room which smelt strongly of alcohol. Three bleary eyed men began to examine the cut. 'Stishes are needed,' slurred one ominously and the others nodded vigorously. 'Lesh get shtarted,' he added.

The trio took several minutes to thread a needle with cat-gut, only achieving the result when two held the needle and the other steered a wavy line towards it with the gut. There was a cheer as their efforts succeeded. 'Doeshnt need a local – hold him shtill,' the sergeant in charge ordered drunkenly.

I watched with horror as the curved needle flickered towards my flesh. First one side of the wound was punctured then the other. The cat-gut seemed a yard long and the pain was agonising as it was slowly drawn through my skin and pulled tight. Three times they repeated the manoeuvre. I guess they knew what I was up to. But my painful ploy worked. I missed the exercise and made my leave.

As time went on I got more and more unsettled with army life. I wanted to do what I wanted when I wanted, and receiving orders was getting more and more irksome. So I decided to extend the leave.

I took a friend with me for a long weekend at my parents' home in Ottery St Mary. A sawmill and factory, a few shops and some pubs huddle at the bend of a river. A short walk and you can see the town. Its only claim to fame was the annual carnival on November 5th when flaming barrels were thrown into the streets.

Our 78-hour pass was soon over but when my mate caught the

bus back to camp he travelled alone – and I kept his Post Office book! I'd been looking after it for him and he had not asked for it to be returned. I drew some money out and spent the remainder of the day in the pub. That night I slept rough.

As I was coming out of the public toilets after my wash and brush up the following morning a policeman stopped me and took me to the police station. When they searched me the Post Office book was found and the recent withdrawal noted. 'Whose book is this?' asked an officer. 'I don't know,' I lied. Something exploded against my cheek. 'Alright, I'll tell you,' I said quickly, changing my mind before another slap came my way. I was offered the chance of returning to the camp in custody, or under my own steam. I agreed to the latter.

'That was a pretty silly thing to do,' said the police sergeant giving me a pep talk as he wrote out a railway warrant. 'People won't always give you a chance, so take the one you've got, go back to camp and make a go of it.'

A police car took me to Exeter Station and I caught the train to camp.

My mate seemed to accept my story that I had only borrowed his money, and intended to return it. I didn't feel guilty, only embarrassed that other people knew.

From then on I was in and out of trouble regularly; rarely anything serious, just carelessness over kit or drill, and a half-hearted attitude. Because I rarely spent much I put the one pound and ten shillings I received each week to work. Since most of the lads were always short of money I lent them cash – with interest. My profits started to mount.

A move to Taunton in Somerset only heightened my irresponsibility. The camp was better, our wooden huts were spread out over a vast area, and there was a choice of meals at the canteen and more entertainment.

By now I had been absent without leave on a few occasions and had committed many petty thefts. But my disdain for army life really boiled up one day on the parade ground.

I refused to obey an order. The junior sergeant was one of the lads I had come in with and we never got on well. Somehow taking orders from him was too much for a sixteen year old finding it difficult to bend to authority. Red in the face he called over the sergeant. 'Look son, just obey this order and we'll say no more about it,' the sergeant soothed. I refused.

This was my first time in the guardroom at Taunton and I found it very different from the old familiar haunt at Bordon. This was a wooden hut in contrast to Bordon's brick. It was brighter, too, having ordinary windows in contrast to Bordon's cell-like apertures. Vertical metal bars were the only concession to security.

I pleaded guilty to the charge – refusing to obey an order – and hardly listened as the major lectured me. 'We have studied your record and it would seem that you are not fitting into the army way of life. This is to be your last chance.' The sentence was 28 days, two weeks loss of pay and the loss of a month's leave.

After only two days I began to talk with the other three men in my cell about the possibility of breaking out. Three of us felt it was worth a try but the fourth, with only a few days to serve, refused to come.

In the middle of the night I clambered up to the window and took hold of one bar with two hands; put a foot against the next bar and heaved. Gradually a gap creaked open, wide enough to climb through.

Once outside the three of us crawled along the grass at the side of the hut. We were quite near to the entrance where guards were on duty wielding pick handles. But they didn't spot us and we crept to our own barrack room. I grabbed some civilian clothes to the 'good luck' wishes of the few friends who were awake and then we scrambled over the fence and started walking along the road. Before long we came to a parked car. One of the lads claimed he could drive, so for three miles we swerved all over the road with the engine roaring, never rising above the second gear. It was no real surprise when our wild ride attracted the attention of police.

We spent the night in the police cells and, after being charged with the offences relating to the stolen car, were returned to camp the following day. The guardroom sergeant hadn't even noticed we were missing!

From then on we were handcuffed to our cell beds. In the morning I was led on what was becoming a ritual parade: to stand stiffly to attention on a little woven mat facing three officers in the commanding officer's room.

'This is the end of the line for you, Private Ralls. When you have finished your sentence you will await the court appearance and after that you will be discharged as unsuitable.'

As he spoke the major detected the smirk twitching along my mouth.

'If you had been a year older you would have been dishonourably discharged, or even sent to prison,' he barked.

'You three have the dubious distinction of being the first to break out of this guardroom. It is a pity that the energy you have for doing wrong could not have been channelled into something good.' The rest of the sentence passed in the tight routine of the guardroom until, after a few weeks back with the platoon, an officer came to see me. 'Your court appearance is next week, Ralls,' he told me. 'When they ask us if we want you back into the army we will say "No." Your discharge papers will be sent to you. You're on your way.'

4: 'Keep your nose clean'

One year has nearly passed since we first met at Exeter Crown Court. We must consider it one of God's wonderful incidents to meet up later . . . if a person wants to change I am convinced this place can be the making of them because Andrew (the chaplain) really does work so hard.

P. Onley Youth Custody Centre

I was still only sixteen so I appeared before the Juvenile Court at Taunton. The room was light and modern and the atmosphere less formal than the major's office. Once again I was facing three people, but this time magistrates. I peered round the room and found it hard to realise that part of my future was about to be decided. It was almost an anti-climax to be remanded for a week.

The remand home at Langport was set in the country, a grey stone house with a short gravel drive, surrounded by lovely gardens. There were no bars at the windows. The khaki shorts which I had to wear felt strange, although we were given long trousers on Sundays for the walk to church.

Smoking was forbidden so I used rose leaves and cigarette ends collected on walks to try and satisfy my craving. More often than not they made me sick – but I kept trying.

The week's remand stretched to twenty-one days before my case came up again. In the meantime days were taken up with household chores and gardening jobs. We walked or played games in the afternoon, and in the evening were allowed to play indoor games before bedtime at nine. Once my parents came to visit me – an awkward occasion with all three of us having little to say. They couldn't understand why I was so rebellious, and I couldn't explain it, even to myself.

When my case did come up I was sentenced to between nine months and two years in an approved school and I returned to the remand home to await allocation.

Sick at the thought of the future it didn't matter to me what happened so I made immediate plans for an escape. With no bars it was simple. A boy from Taunton accompanied me when I left one night after lights out. We were going to look odd in shorts so I climbed on to the guttering and edged my way along the roof to the window of the laundry room where the long trousers were kept. The window opened easily. Within seconds I was down the drainpipe clutching a couple of pairs of trousers and we were away.

We reckoned the easiest way to get to Taunton was to follow the railway track so we did, jumping to one side regularly as trains roared out of the darkness. It seemed to take hours.

In Taunton we went to my mate's house and his mother gave us breakfast. We'd hardly finished when the police called – not entirely unexpectedly. So we climbed into the tiny loft. Since it was only a single storey asbestos building the loft was no more than three feet high at its highest. We lay sweating and listening to the voices of the policemen a few inches below us. Soon I was itching and scratching – the loft was lined with fibreglass! It took days for the minute particles to disappear from my flesh.

When the police had gone the friend's mother gave us money and we left.

It was a hot summer day and with the heat, and the fragments of fibreglass irritating me all over it was difficult to keep from scratching. We needed money and my mate knew someone who would buy bicycles. We saw two lying against a wall. 'How about these?' he said. I was scared stiff but said casually, 'Yeah, why not,' jumped on one and rode off. I was several yards down the road when he realised what had happened.

'Wait for me,' he yelled, grabbed the other bike and pedalled furiously after me.

We went to a wood where we intended to wait until night. Later my accomplice went off to sell the bicycles and joined me in the early evening bringing food and drink. It was getting dark as we made plans to buy train tickets to London with the thought of trying to get aboard a ship for America.

A loud-hailer interrupted our reverie. 'Come out and give yourselves up,' it boomed. Headlights pierced the darkness.

We crouched, swearing and edged backwards into a cornfield which bounded the woods, running in different directions. After about fifty yards I dropped flat, crawling through the high corn, my heart beating frantically. Torch beams swept the darkness. I pressed my face into the ground and lay still trying not to breathe. A padding noise grew louder and a weight bore down on my back. I twisted and looked up into the panting jaws of a slobbering alsatian dog pulling at the leash held by a towering dark shape waving a torch.

My twenty-four hours of freedom had ended.

'Once more and you'll be in prison,' the headmaster warned.

A few weeks later I escaped again. This time I made it to Bristol and was free for a week before being recaptured. My hatred of authority was growing.

To halt my adventures bars were fitted to the windows of all the bedrooms in the remand home but since they were wrought iron they not only bent easily but eventually broke. So a week after my return I was on the run again, my final fling before being sent to St Swithins Approved School on the Isle of Wight.

I decided to return to the army camp to look up a few old friends. I climbed over the fence and crept into the old barracks room, avoiding soldiers when I saw them. I tapped on the window to attract attention but there was no response. Cautiously I peered over the sill, surprised to see no-one there.

The building was deserted. The thought struck me: they must be on an exercise. I slipped round the front and into the old familiar room with a feeling of nostalgia. I was trying to work out what to do next when, through the window, I spotted someone going past who had joined up at the same time as myself. I attracted his attention and he came below the sill. 'I'm on the run. I haven't eaten since this morning and could do with some food,' I told him. Reluctantly he agreed to help.

In the early evening he returned, tapping on the window before passing a metal tray through. 'Look, don't hang around, you'll get caught,' he warned, anxious for himself as much as me.

I ate and then curled up on one of the bunks for a few minutes.

Crash! I woke suddenly. The sun was blazing through the windows and I could hear the heavy tread of boots in the passage at the end of the building. I jumped from the bed, hastily straightened the blankets, and slipped underneath the iron frame, holding my breath. Two pairs of boots clonked into view. From the conversation I gathered it was an officer and a sergeant. They wandered up and down talking loudly for several agonising minutes before leaving.

It was the middle of the morning. I was stuck until night. I lit a cigarette and elected to rest until dark, trusting that my former colleagues would not return. They didn't. As light faded I went to work on their lockers. Two reasonable sized suitcases were easily put to one side and then I filled them. Most of the money I discovered was in Post Office books; I stacked about thirty of them into one of the cases for future use. I selected some shaving gear, tucked that into a case and sat down to wait for darkness.

As soon as it was dark I got out of the back of the camp and caught a bus to Taunton carrying the suitcases like a jaunty holidaymaker. I had decided to go to my parents' house and get some of my own things so from Taunton I caught a train to Exeter and a bus from there to West Hill.

That night I slept in the woods overlooking my parents' house. From my vantage point lying in the dew-soaked grass I watched them leave for work the following morning before making my way down the hill, smashing a window and entering the house.

It seemed strange stealing my own things but when I had made my choice I felt good. I had everything together at last. Now I was ready to face the future.

I left the bus at the Black Horse, a transport cafe on the A30 between Honiton and Exeter. Lorries trundled past regularly for all parts of the country and I needed a lift. First I ate, and poked a few coins into the fruit machine just to test my luck, then I went outside and stood by the road jerking my thumb to win attention. A huge red lorry chugged to a halt.

'Where are you off to, then?' I asked.

'Perth,' the driver replied.

'That will do,' I said and climbed into the cab. The engine roared powerfully as the driver kicked it through the gears.

I was on my way. 'You've done it,' I congratulated myself. 'Money, clothes, Post Office books, and an open road.' Perched high in the cab the world was at my feet.

It took three days to get to Perth and during that time I slept in the cab at nights. As we halted at different towns I cashed another of the Post Office books – none contained much but it gave me a steady supply of cash.

Eventually we pulled into a transport cafe on the outskirts of Perth and I had a last meal with the driver in a large wooden-floored cafe packed with drivers and their mates. When I could put off departure no longer I shook hands with my friend of three days and left to take up my position alongside a bus stop.

Knowing no-one and having no idea of the geography of the area I got off the bus somewhere in the country and spent that evening under a hedge. When I woke it was dawn, the sun was beginning to filter across the fields and through the trees. With no plans and no commitments I felt a tremendous sense of well being. I boarded the first bus that came and rode into town to hunt for a cafe . . . somewhere to eat and also kill time.

In the afternoon I went to the cinema. It was there that a man approached me. He sidled up to me and whispered, 'On the run, mate?' My heart sank. I was convinced he was a plain clothed detective.

He wasn't. Just a man who had spotted me with my suitcases and put two-and-two together and made it add up to a criminal! Gratefully I accepted his offer of somewhere to stay – the Post Office books wouldn't last forever and I needed accommodation and another source of income.

Jock, that was his name, had a huge alsatian dog and had been in trouble himself. He was, in fact, the district's tough-man. For some weeks things went well. I had money and managed to contribute something towards my food and he was delighted when I offered to take the dog out for a walk on the local heath (called the Inch). The rest of the time I hung around cafes or sat in the cinema.

One unpleasant incident should have sounded warning bells in my mind but I was so enamoured with freedom that it didn't register. I woke one night to find Jock drunk and in bed with me with rather obvious intentions. Somehow I managed to put him off and he never tried again but it was when my money ran out that the crunch came.

Jock suggested a homosexual friend would be willing to give me money if I was ready to oblige him. The thought sickened me but I didn't seem to have any choice so that evening I went along to the flat to which Jock had directed me.

A group of young blokes were in there with an older man drinking and chatting. I joined in. As time went on they drifted off in pairs until I was left with the older man.

I followed instructions, got paid a small amount, and agreed to call back the next day. Inside I felt sick and determined somehow to pay him back. I didn't like homosexuals. I did return the next day, but a lot earlier than agreed, knowing he would be out. Cracking open the gas meter I helped myself to the money and selected several other items from the flat. 'This is the real pay-off,' I thought as I scooped up the coins, slipping the other goods into my pockets.

That afternoon I was in a cafe with some of the local youngsters I had got to know when two men came in asking for me. There was nothing I could do and as they looked in my direction and confidently headed towards me I knew I was finished. At the Police Station they searched me and discovered the items I had stolen. They wanted to know where I lived and when I told them they looked at each other, each flashing the same peculiar smile.

'So you're the new lad, eh?' one said. 'How old are you?'

'Sixteen and a half.'

'You've ended up in a right state.' I was charged and put in the cells overnight. Next day I appeared before the Sheriff's Court where checks revealed I was wanted in England. Freedom had ended again.

For a week I was remanded in Perth Prison in a cell overlooking the detention centre next door. I spent my time watching the men digging holes and pushing wheel-barrows.

Then, after the usual salt-porridge breakfast I was given my kit and taken to the reception area. Immediately I recognised a tall figure as the man who had taken us for games at the remand home.

'So we meet again,' he smiled. 'From what I hear arrest

is the best thing that could happen to you.' Some greeting.

He slipped a handcuff over my right wrist, clicking it to so that it pinched my flesh and then fastening the other end to his left wrist. Escape was to be impossible. We were driven in a police car to the railway station. As the train pulled out I thought, 'I'll come back here when I get out' . . . but I never did.

It was a strange feeling being handcuffed, people gave us sly glances and I longed to say to them, 'I'm taking him in.'

I asked my escort where we were going. 'Exeter Prison,' he replied.

'Then what?'

'You'll go to court again for the offences which occurred after you left us and I expect you'll go back to prison until you are ready for the approved school.' It was a bleak prospect.

For the rest of the journey we talked of ordinary things, about certain lads I knew at the remand home, football results, and other mundane subjects. All the time I reflected on the good time I had enjoyed at the home – afternoon games in the sunshine, walks and indoor games. I would miss those. But it was no use looking back. Life had to go on. I'd always seemed to get through.

'Another trip out, eh Ralls?' I was greeted by the same guy who had brought me back from Scotland some weeks earlier. This time we were heading for the Isle of Wight and after the weeks I spent in Exeter Prison I was looking forward to the journey. The only thing that broke the monotony of life in Exeter had been being able to see girls from the women's wing across the yard.

Once on the train there were a lot of pretty girls around as well as the sights and sounds of the countryside. But best of all was to eat food which had variety, stretch my legs and view different scenery.

The train took us to Lymington and from there we went by car across the ferry to the Isle of Wight. St Swithins was a few miles from Yarmouth and by the time we arrived it was early afternoon.

About half a mile up from the sea a drive swept in boldly from the road revealing a large spread-out building with gardens on the right. Inside we went past heavy, dark oak furniture in a huge clean-smelling hall before rounding a corner into the recreation room.

A couple of lads were playing snooker and others lounged around. I spotted the dining room on the left and we went through another door into a long passage punctuated by doors at regular intervals. Most were to baths or toilets but halfway down was the entrance to the sewing room and a stairway to the dormitories.

After this brief inspection I was given a meal and led to the sewing room to get my clothes. My guide was a prisoner soon due for discharge – excited at the thought of leaving.

Time was moving on and I had to see the headmaster so I pulled on a pair of shorts, clutched the rest of my clothes and was taken to the dormitory and allocated a bed – one of twenty or so. The view over the drive was a pleasant change from that in prison and the bright, neat room a relief from the drabness of the cell.

I scrambled into a shirt and left the rest of my clothes tipped on the bed when I was bustled in front of the headmaster. He belonged to one of the Orders of Brothers in charge of the centre. Dressed in a black cassock which didn't strike me as strange because I had been used to it at my Roman Catholic School, his eyes bored into me as I stood before his desk. 'You have quite a record for one so young,' he said pausing for my reaction. 'If you attempt to escape just once you will go to a very different place.' He paused again. 'This school is run by brothers and lay helpers. You will call the brothers "Brother" and the lay helpers "Sir". For the first few weeks you will be on cleaning duties but as time goes on you will earn the chance to do something different.

'If you wish you can learn various trades or, since we are partly a nautical school, you can learn about the Merchant Navy and join directly from here on your discharge.

'Keep your nose clean and your stay should be quite enjoyable. We are not a Borstal but if you mess around you will find yourself in one pretty quickly.'

With that I was dismissed and escorted back to the billiard room where everyone was waiting for dinner.

The oblong dining tables seated four on each side with the head of the table dishing out the food for each group of nine – good if he were fair-minded, not so good otherwise. I was fortunate. Like most institutions for young offenders St Swithins was run on a tie system – when you first arrived you got a certain colour tie but after a while got upgraded to the next colour and an accompanying slight rise in pay. Each day we were given marks out of five for work and also for conduct and on these marks depended how much we were paid and how soon we were upgraded.

Another institutional tradition was that of share-mates. Each person had one particular friend who shared all that came to both of them. A lot of time would be spent together and each one helped the other when necessary. It seemed to work well. I had three such mates during my time there. I fitted into the daily routine, deciding to do the time and get it over with. There were few breaks in the monotony.

I had one run-in with a guy called Lewis after things sparked in the laundry room near the bottom of the stairs. I had been in a few punch-ups in the army but didn't really know how to handle myself so when words led to blows I kept getting knocked down. Something told me it was important to keep getting up and coming back – I was willing to have a go if nothing else.

Neither of us was badly hurt but it inspired me to join the boxing team to discover more about the finer arts of using my fists.

A year went by and I had earned a bit of respect in the school for being someone not to be messed around – a hard nut.

Trips outside broke the boredom and I particularly enjoyed the outings on the whalers, the school's large boats powered by a row of 15 foot oars. That led me to put my name down to join the Merchant Navy until, after going home on leave near the end of my time in the school, I changed my mind.

I was beginning to question many things. My parents were loving but I felt distant from them. Their Roman Catholic faith didn't seem to provide anything to help, even attending all the compulsory services at St Swithins didn't seem to answer the questions which hammered around inside my teenage mind.

One bright spot arrived late one afternoon in the shape of Billy Donoghue whom I used to serve mass with all those years before. It was a relief to have a friend from the past but the future was beckoning. I looked forward to getting out but felt a tingle of fear . . . my tomorrows were so uncertain. When I was released I breathed a sigh of relief, another stage in life was over. I had survived. But the tingle still remained.

5: Floating with the current

I'm in here for arson. I set fire to my bed-sit 2½ years ago. I was on remand at Holloway for five months which was very bad. I prayed and prayed then.I came here and pray here as well. Well, I used to. Funnily enough just lately I haven't been praying at all well as the medicine I take at night really knocks me out, and during the day I'm either too busy or otherwise involved in something. This upsets me as I really would love to pray properly but don't know how. I love Jesus and God but with all my troubles my head is always so mixed up. They say it's a miracle I'm still alive, especially when I threw myself off a 150ft cliff and got away with a bad headache.

M. Broadmoor Hospital

After leaving approved school I stayed for a few weeks with my parents at Ottery St Mary but life was dull. They were having a bungalow built and sometimes I helped the builders; more often than not, however, I drifted into Sidmouth where there was more action. On Saturdays Billy Donoghue and I would go to the local dances and pick up girls. At other times we met in our local pub, The London, where we were ready for anything after a couple of drinks. Before opening time we spent our time in Tansilles, a chip shop with tables at the rear.

Sidmouth is a quiet unspoilt seaside town with little to do, particularly in the winter when the sea smashes against the sea wall, rattling the shingle, and the wind seems to slice through anything. But summer was something different . . . the girls arrived from every quarter, the French first and later in the season the Swedish.

Billy was an Elvis Presley fan who dressed like his idol whenever he could with smart, flashy clothes. He had the ability to string words together in a way which acted like magnets to the girls, unfortunately that same asset drew the attention of many guys and led to a number of fights. My parents didn't approve of Billy; but since his didn't care for me it almost guaranteed we would remain firm friends. Our friendship often took us to the Black Horse, an all-night cafe near Exeter, and on other occasions we gate-crashed youth clubs in the area to play table tennis or cards.

It was through a game of cards that I met Fred Broom. Fred was a local lad, a painter – of buildings not canvas – with a big reputation as a tough guy. It was a friendship that was to outlive my kinship with Billy and develop in an unusual way in later years. Tough as he was Fred was good to me, something seemed to spark between us that was right.

Before long, the flexible hours I was keeping led to a series of squabbles at home that annoyed me so I moved into Sidmouth and stayed with a young couple. Bill and I were out of work so there was plenty of time and that led to a growing need for money. I wanted to look up some friends in London so, lacking the fare, the decision was made: Billy and I would break into a seafront cafe in Sidmouth.

The cafe backed on to a cricket club and it was simplicity itself to scramble on to the roof and almost as easy to force open the skylight. Once inside our luck was out. There was little to take but a few pounds inside the fruit machine. With a pocket that chinked with loose change I thumbed a lift to the Black Horse and from there to London.

I stayed with a woman Bill had recommended and slept with her. She was not the greatest looker in the world but life could have ticked along nicely if I hadn't mentioned that one fact in a letter to a girl in Sidmouth. Unfortunately I asked one of the children belonging to the girl to post the letter; instead the child opened it, read it, and reported my views to her mother. I left quickly!

The contents of the till in a cafe in the area funded me for the return to Devon and I arrived at the Black Horse in the early hours of the morning, playing the machines until daylight broke. Catching a bus to Ottery St Mary I stopped in a local shop to change some of the bags of coins for notes – my mistake.

A couple of miles from the shop the bus I was travelling on was stopped by the police and I was taken to Sidmouth, charged with breaking into the cafes in Sidmouth and London, and sentenced to three months' detention. Actually that pleased me. I had heard that Fred was in detention for slashing a bloke across the throat with a razor. He'd been lucky to have the charge dropped from attempted murder to grievous bodily harm so I waited for my escort from the police station after the hearing thinking, 'At least I shall know someone there.'

The wire perimeter fence seemed to go on for miles. And the grim interior was a visual reminder of my introduction to the centre – 'It's tough here, and we'll crack down on you if you step out of line by so much as an inch.' The haircut I was given reinforced that ideal: it was shorter than even the army style, leaving just a tuft at the back of my head. I was made to bath before being given clothes and taken to the dormitory area. Everywhere I went I had to run . . . I was beginning to regret getting caught.

Another indication of the harsh code occurred when I spotted Fred kneeling scrubbing a floor. A broad wink was all that even that hard character dared give me. The routine was tight and regimented. I was up at 5.30 in the morning and given half a cup of cocoa before going to the parade ground for thirty minutes of physical training. Three officers stood round as we were forced to run round the yard stopping on command to perform press-ups or other exercises.

It was winter and the cold would seep into every part of my body. The rest of the day brought a regular routine of work or more physical exercise. In the gymnasium was the circuit which I loathed. Apparatus was spread like torture equipment along the route; weights to lift, ropes to climb, a bench to step on and off. And all the while instead of things becoming easier through regular use I merely progressed to a harder circuit.

We were not allowed to smoke – an ideal rule for encouraging us to give up smoking. One day Fred and I found half a cigarette and it made us feel sick and dizzy.

The evenings were taken up with classes and recreation – table tennis, reading books or just talking. Only the weekends were different. Saturday evenings found us preparing for the weekly inspection, polishing floors, shoes, and every bit of brass there was available. Five o'clock on Sunday morning we were roused to put the finishing touches to everything – no wrinkles in the bed and the rooms neat and sparkling. And always after breakfast the morning service at church.

It was one of those days when, exhausted with work and frustrated with life, I flung myself on my bed and asked myself, 'What am I doing here? Life seems to carry me along on a current which is so strong I can't resist it. Occasionally I get washed up on a bleak shore, spend a few months in custody only to be carried off on another tide of circumstance.'

There were two good pointers: I was put in a work party with Fred which drew us still closer together, and the constant exercise toughened me up.

When release day came I grabbed my clothes from the reception room, changed and bounced into the world ready to take on anything once again.

Even the new bungalow my parents were now living in couldn't tempt me to stay at home more than a few weeks. We were drawing further apart – so was my liking for work.

Life became one long round of hanging about in Sidmouth and finishing off the evenings in the pubs or on the seafront. For a time I slept in the village hall, slipping in through a window at night, using the cooker to create an evening meal, and leaving by the window early in the morning. Bill moved in with me for a time and friends brought us food. I ranged from job to job: picking tomatoes in a nursery, working in a hotel, and even installing the STD system in the telephone exchange which was simple enough – matching coloured wires – but wasn't well paid.

The fact that it didn't pay much led Bill and I to the local Anglican church. We were easing some of the lead off a window pane when a sudden noise and the flash of a torch made us run like mad. Bill dropped behind a gravestone to avoid detection and I finished up in the park on the other side of the town under some bushes. I gave it a few hours and made my way back to Bill's flat. It had scared me. I didn't fancy being caught again.

Now I was cleaning windows and with Fred out of detention enjoyed his company along with Bill's. I also found somewhere to live, staying with a family on the nearby council estate.

Bill and I worked out a system of cheating at cards and began to clean up in pubs and flats around town. Our system of kicks under the table kept us on top. The only night we had serious trouble was when we were playing some Italians and they became suspicious when the kitty built up while we were on top. I slipped a knife from my belt and they withdrew their objection. They didn't play with us again, though.

It was summer and the hot nights were an invitation to climb the wall of one hotel for an uninvited swimming session in the hotel pool . . . or we would rove along the seafront.

I ditched my latest occupation, a chimney sweep, for life in a hotel making sandwiches and afternoon teas. It freed me for the evenings and meant I could sleep late in the mornings, that is unless I got up for an early morning swim with the Swedish girls – a Scandinavian habit they seemed to enjoy.

I lost my job in the hotel and moved into digs in town. But that led me to another source of cash. The husband in the house always had a wallet packed with notes. Late one night I discovered well over £100 so I took five or ten pounds occasionally and he didn't seem to notice.

Over-confident, I peeled off £50 in notes one night and the next morning he called me into the front room. 'Some money is missing and I am going to search your room,' he threatened. He went all over the room and found nothing. Then he decided to search me. The money was pinned to the back of my underpants so I stood as his hands flickered all over me . . . leaving the money undetected. I was scared, though, and later left, shouting he had picked on me because of my record.

Bill and I shared a flat we had moved into over a launderette which was ideal – we could take our girl-friends back there with no bother.

I decided to break into the council house I had lived in, knowing where the money was kept. Two bulldogs who were always slobbering about didn't worry me and sure enough when I climbed in through a window at four in the morning they made snorting noises of welcome. I opened the cupboard where I knew the cash was kept and scooped the lot. Obviously I would be suspect number one so I gave the money to a friend, 'on loan.' When the police called at my work and searched me they found only a ten shilling note. My friend presented me with the money a bit at a time.

I had got out of detention in April and Fred had met a girl called Wendy after his release and started going steady with her. She was an attractive girl and in November they were planning to get married.

It made me stop and think but I decided to continue with my love-them and leave-them existence. There were other exciting interludes. I decided to join the Mods and Rockers at Hastings. Packing leather jackets and smart clothes, so that I could do a quick change act and fit in with whichever gang was on top, I made my way to Hastings. I roamed the streets for hours with some mates following the gangs but always missed the trouble. It was all a bit of a let-down, especially when I read in the newspapers of the riots that had missed me by minutes.

So it was back to Devon where my luck was still out. When Fred and I broke into an office one night the knife slipped and cut me. I was also getting violent, one night smashing one guy in the face until blood ran everywhere. I was quite cocky about that until a few nights later when his mate, a bigger guy, trapped me in the toilet and I ended up with my face in the urinal!

With Christmas approaching I went to the Christmas Eve dance – the only Christmas I was to have outside prison for some years. Bill and I danced, spent the evening with some girls, and then decided to enlarge our wardrobe.

We broke into a clothing shop through a side window and carried armfuls of clothes back to our flat before returning to the dance. We had a third fellow with us but he was so scared he insisted on wearing all he stole – so he went to the dance in six T-shirts, three shirts, and two pairs of trousers. He soaked the lot in sweat while Bill and I laughed at his discomfort.

Tough as I was I sometimes needed a little extra support, so I got it in the form of knives, a studded belt or a lump of wood. One night Fred, Bill and I knew a fight was in the air so I prepared in advance. Fred and Wendy watched me shave all the bristles off a hair brush until it was ready for the battle. That evening I pulled on a leather glove, took the hairless brush and when I spotted a couple of blokes laying into Fred cracked one over the head with it. The brush broke, the end flying across the dance-floor, and the man dropped like a stone. In the confusion that followed a girl grabbed the pair of us and hustled us back to the flat in her car.

Fred was always a steady worker and decided to buy a car. Bill and I went to Honiton with him to get the vehicle and watched him drive his first car with pride. He'd driven a mile or so when steam started to pour from the bonnet. The radiator was empty, and cracked. From then on we carried a five gallon drum of water. Having transport was luxury. We could make it to the Black Horse late at night with our girls.

Bill was working making bird tables and I was the only one now out of work. Having three girl friends at the same time was something of a drain on my meagre financial resources so we decided on a couple of 'jobs'.

First on the list was a mobile delivery van. We had seen one point on the delivery route where the driver parked the van and had a long walk to the house to which he was delivering. With Fred as our getaway driver we were to wait until the man was on his way, drive up, grab all we could and drive off. Things didn't work out. When the time came to start the car it wouldn't go – the radiator was empty – and by the time we had filled it the van had gone!

We fared no better at our next stop, a sub-post office. Bill eased up the window while Fred was filling up the radiator in the car. As Bill slid through the window there was an almighty crash. We ran for the car. It refused to start again. Fortunately it chonked into life after we jump-started it and we drove towards Sidmouth.

Bill had a third idea. 'The mobile shop in Ottery,' he suggested. The shop-cum-van was parked in a garage but ripping a hole in the roof of the garage was easy. There was no money but lots of food and cigarettes so we bundled them into the back of the car and arrived back at the flat about three in the morning.

Our girls were there so we dumped the stuff on the floor and Bill and I had a big fry-up before sleeping. A couple of hours later I was awakened by a knock on the door.

'Come in Fred,' I said blearily opening the door. It wasn't Fred – it was the police.

Fred was to join us later at the police station. The police had been watching us for days, they said, and had seen us unload all the stolen stuff and waited until we had settled down.

At Ottery St Mary court we were handcuffed together to hear the magistrates remand us for a week. We were then loaded into a Black Maria and taken to Exeter Remand Home. Rubbing our fingers and thumbs on the ink blocks to have our fingerprints taken was second nature, as was not smiling for the photographs. But Bill couldn't control his sense of humour. 'One postcard size for me mum,' he grinned after the photographic session.

We were taken to stand in front of a desk in the newly built remand wing for young prisoners. Behind the desk the officer looked curt and unsympathetic.

'Broom,' he barked.

'Yes sir.'

'Ralls.'

'Yes sir.'

'Donoghue,' he continued and we waited with bated breath.

'That's me,' Bill called back.

'Sir, Donoghue, Sir,' snapped the officer.

'No need to call me sir – Bill will do.'

Crash. Bill was knocked to the floor muttering, 'Where's your sense of humour?'

Time passed quickly, alternating between sawing wood, cleaning the cells and landings, and being locked up at night. We had another remand before our case was passed on to Exeter Quarter Sessions. My life of crime was progressing me upwards through the legal system.

A Black Maria took us to the Quarter Sessions in the heart of Exeter. I didn't know what to expect. It was very different from the magistrates' court I was used to – men dressed in black robes and wearing curly wigs scurried about carrying rolls of paper wrapped in pink tape. A coat of arms hung on the wall behind the Recorder, sitting on his own, his face devoid of any expression. I could see my parents at the back of the court, and my probation officer, but I was more concerned at putting on a show for Bill's girlfriend, Veronica, whom I had spotted in the public seats. We each pleaded guilty and listened as our lawyers pleaded for light sentences. Then the probation officers passed round their reports. As I studied a copy of mine any hopes I had of escaping with a light sentence disappeared. I read the final paragraph. It recommended Borstal.

We stood and listened as the verdicts were announced. 'Broom this is your first offence for stealing. You have a steady job and are getting married. The court sees fit to give you a chance.' Fred breathed a sigh of relief as he was given three years on probation.

Bill was sent to a detention centre for three months with the words 'I hope a good sharp sentence will teach you a lesson.'

My turn had come. 'Ralls you have quite a record. It seems you were the leading light in most of the offences brought before the court. You have been punished before but don't seem prepared to learn. You will go to Borstal for a term of not less than nine months and not more than two years. There you will learn something that will help you change the course that you are on in this life.'

I didn't really hear most of it. The significant part had sunk in – nine months at least.

'See you, mate,' said Fred as he was led away. I didn't answer. I couldn't afford to be seen to be soft, though I was near to tears.

Down in the cells Dad passed me some cigarettes without saying a word. Mum had been crying. What could we say to each other.?

The dull ache began to pass with the days. One morning I was given my own clothes and ushered into a mini-bus with a few other lads. We were handcuffed together and the bus turned towards Exeter Prison.

Later that night I cracked, and smashed my cell breaking the windows and furniture, barricading myself in and half-heartedly attempting to cut my wrists. The screws managed to break in and put me in a padded cell. I was naked and fed on bread and water for three days before being shipped to London's Wormwood Scrubs before being allocated to a Borstal. It was like being a parcel, tossed around until I finally reached the correct destination.

I began to wonder where that would be. I had tried the army cells, remand homes, approved school and even Exeter Prison. What would Borstal be like?

6: Borstal boy

I have been away from Portland Borstal for almost eight months now and because I decided to walk with God my life has a new meaning. I would like to thank you, Tony, for the help that you gave me while I was in Portland. I have got a steady job as painter and decorator and more recently have been promoted to foreman with younger boys working under me. So you can see people are trusting me again. Now the Lord is with me there is no way I will ever let him go.

K. Portsmouth

I sat in the inevitable pre-admission bath, flipped the soap around the white enamelled sides and felt impressed. The sheer size of Wormwood Scrubs daunted me. It was like a city with rolling lawns, a church and all kinds of buildings dotted around. In Exeter Prison all the wings met in the centre, circling a huge spiral staircase. Here the wings were separate buildings.

Bath over, it was the allocation room and the news that I was to be in D Wing. The wing was filled with the usual prison smell of disinfectant fighting a losing battle over the pervading stench of urine. Wire netting ran like a rabbit-run alongside the landings and over the well between to prevent suicides, or objects being thrown on people below. And all the time there was noise . . . shouting, walking, and the clanging of doors. On the ground floor the black flagstones in the centre spread away to endless cell doors ranged on either side.

I stood in my Borstal outfit clutching blankets and a small card indicating my religion. Red for Roman Catholics, white for Church of England or blue for non-Conformists. Mine was red. It also listed my offences and the date of my sentence.

A screw came and accompanied me to my cell, high up on a

top landing. Keys jangled as he opened the door. My red card was deposited in a worn wooden rack outside the door so that anyone could read who I was and what I had done. I put my gear on the bed and wandered back along the corridor to the toilets. The cell had a metal pot for the calls of nature overnight and early in the morning it had to be slopped out in a giant basin in the toilets. With a hundred or so inmates pouring their waste away it was a terrible stink first thing in the morning.

On the landing I bumped into some of the other lads who had been driven in with me. They had already discovered we would be in the Scrubs two or three months while the authorities decided where we would be going. Back in the cell I lay on the bed and suddenly felt very lost. What was life all about? All I could think of was how lucky I was: my cell had a wooden floor, much warmer than the stone floors in other cells.

The next morning the governor repeated the news I had picked up the previous night: we were to be assessed and passed on to the appropriate Borstal. It was spring and the march to the governor's office was pleasant alongside the grass. Different prisoners were spotted, some wearing red armbands, others blue – an indication they were trusted to walk round without supervision.

Otherwise it was the usual dull routine, punctuated only by a film show or, since I was a Catholic, a trip to church on Sunday which made a break but did little else for me. The monotony led to depression, and one day my mind snapped as I was on the landing. A little guy threatened me and in a second we were fighting. As I charged in there was a sudden flash and my vision went completely, pain stabbing my eyes. I discovered later he had rammed his forefinger and middle finger into my eyes. Blind, I grabbed him and pulled him to me while I shook my head clear. I thumped my right fist forward towards his chin when a screw yanked us apart. 'Shake and forget it,' we were told. I did but made a mental note to get the little guy some day, though I never got the chance.

The day came when I was called before the governor. 'Ralls you are leaving us tomorrow for Dover Borstal. It is a relatively short term place so you could be out in nine months if you behave yourself. Good luck lad.'

The next day it was back into my civilian clothes, on with the handcuffs and through the huge gates en route for Dover, a Borstal Boy.

'Borstal is much better than being in the nick,' I reasoned as the mini-bus reached the outskirts of Dover. 'There's your future accommodation', we were told as a guard pointed up the hill.

I could vaguely make out some buildings at the top. The coach wound its way through the town rising higher as it went and drew up outside the gates. There was a moat with a bridge across it. The moat was about twelve feet deep but free of water I noticed. The bus rolled cautiously over the bridge and turned left down a slight slope towards a building where we were freed from the handcuffs and taken down some steps into the reception area. Almost mechanically I took the new clothing issue and watched as my own clothes were packed away in a cardboard box for at least nine months.

Then I was taken to my house, an underground building approached down more steps. I entered the recreation area first: three barred windows pierced the far wall overlooking the moat. Off to the left and right were archways leading to two dormitories. I was in the right hand one. At the end of the dormitory were more windows, again overlooking the moat. The bed next to mine was occupied by a bloke called Peachy. Later we were to become share-mates. I was given a blue tie indicating I was new. Red ties followed after a month, then green and finally orange when a discharge date was given.

I fancied becoming a painter but was made to do a couple of weeks on a general working party. I was set to work in the moat digging and clearing different stone buildings. The whole area had originally been built by French prisoners of war during Napoleon's time.

Saturday and Sunday afternoons were sports times, football in the moat mainly. I was in my house football team and competition between houses was pretty tough.

The longer I worked and played around the moat the more I began to see it as a way of escape. I spent time in the dormitory dreaming as I peered through the window over the moat and schemed. As I worked or played I had half a mind on the job while the other half was racing round the top of the moat looking for possible escape routes. Peachy, a biggish lad who wore glasses, could drive and fancied giving the escape attempt a go. Because he didn't smoke he converted his tobacco ration into money and by borrowing we managed to build up a little fund of money. Our major problem was when to make the break. Night seemed the best, the doors were open and we could move freely to evening classes or go to the gymnasium. Our best route appeared to be to jump into the moat and make for the bridge leading out of the back of the camp. I reckoned I could throw a rope and pull myself up on to a roof alongside the bridge. The rope was a problem, but we solved it on sports day. After the races, Peachy and I grabbed rope used to line the makeshift track and wrapped lengths of it round our bodies under our shirts, taking it back to the house undetected. I managed to find a piece of metal and between us we bent it into a hook shape. We were ready.

Strangely enough I was beginning to fit into the Borstal life, but having made the plans decided to go ahead with the bid for freedom. With a few days to go we began to save food from the canteen. Another lad asked to join us. I wasn't very excited at having him along but realised he was a grass (informer) so decided it was better to take him. That way he wouldn't be so keen to give the game away.

The night arrived. We booked our names down to visit the gym, slid over the bank into the moat and disappeared into its dark patches. Then the rain started. Black, sheets of wetness soaking us through. At the bottom of the bridge I fitted our makeshift hook on to the rope and flipped it up. It caught something. But then I found the rope too wet and slippery to climb, the one eventuality for which I wasn't prepared. Desperate to avoid detection Peachy stood on my shoulders and pulled himself up. I got on the other bloke and with a bit of help from Peachy, above, reached the safety of the bridge. Then we both ran, leaving the other guy in the moat shouting angrily into the rain.

The only thing now stopping us was a high fence with rolled wire at the top. I thought our run was at an end but more by desperation than anything we managed to climb the wire and wriggle between the strands at the top. Later we discovered we could have walked round the fence. We missed it by a few yards! We were soaked but so happy that we danced in the rain, laughing. I clutched a bag of food and spare clothes and we made for the field, already earmarked as our hiding place for the next twentyfour hours. After that the road blocks, which we knew would be set up, should be withdrawn.

We found a clump of trees and tried to sleep in the rain. I woke in the morning to the sound of many feet shuffling around. My heart sunk. I peeped through the foliage and saw the cause of the noise – a herd of cows having their early morning feed, some gazing curiously at us. Luckily it was a sunny day so we laid out some of the spare clothing to dry. I could see the road and in the distance a road block with policemen stopping all cars and questioning the occupants. Towards night the police car drew away.

When it was dark we crossed the road, taking care not to be seen, and discovered a caravan obviously deserted. Inside were a couple of pairs of overalls which we took and pulled over our Borstal shirts and trousers.

It was our hiding place for another day and from it we could overlook a camping site with tents and caravans. The cars parked alongside the colourful tents gave us the idea and when darkness fell again we crept into the camp where Peachy found a mini he thought he would be able to start. Whispering to me to keep watch, he opened the car door and released the bonnet. Every noise he made sounded like an alarm signal. Eventually we were ready. Carefully he eased the bonnet back. It clicked into place, sounding like a pistol shot in the night air. We sat inside and he poked under the dashboard and fiddled with a couple of wires. The engine turned but wouldn't fire. 'Come on, Peachy,' I whispered. Two or three times the engine rumbled, just a few feet from the tent where the owner slept. A fourth time Peachy poked at the wires and the little car thundered into life. We jerked forward before he managed to get it under control, swung across the field over the rutted pathway, through a gate, and on to the road. 'Let's go as far as we can,' I urged. The pocket alongside my passenger seat had some maps inside it so as Peachy jolted us along I tried to direct him along minor roads just in case the police were still keeping their vigil.

Money and cigarettes were conveniently placed under the dashboard so it looked a good ride.

We were still wearing the overalls I had discovered in the caravan but the money we had saved in Borstal and the loose change I found in the car wouldn't last long. I knew that eventually we would need more petrol. Peachy provided the plan. We drove to a petrol station and pulled up alongside the pumps.

'Fill her up, mate,' I told the attendant rattling a few coins in my pocket. 'We're in a hurry.' The attendant topped up the tank and was bending to replace the petrol cap when Peachy poked the car into life, released the clutch, and sent the vehicle skidding across the forecourt and down the road.

We arrived in Sidmouth that night and slept on the common. At four the next morning we drove to Ottery St Mary and broke into the mobile shop, filling our mini's boot with cigarettes and food, before returning to the common. Next day Peachy drove me into Sidmouth to look up a girlfriend. Later in the day I strolled back to our meeting place. As I reached a hill overlooking the car I saw policemen inspecting it and driving Peachy away. 'His freedom didn't last long,' I thought.

I slept the night on the hill overlooking the sea and woke to the sound of seagulls and with the sun in my eyes. The waves were lapping on the beach and for the rest of the morning I lay sunbathing and enjoying my liberty. Fred and Wendy came up to see me during the day, bringing food. Since I had last seen them they had been married and Wendy was pregnant. After another visit to the town for coffee and food I returned to my view and considered my next move.

A voice broke my concentration. 'Right, Mike. Time to give up and go back and do your time.' Sergeant Evans, the policeman who had been instrumental in arresting me on a previous occasion, was behind me with a couple of other officers. 'Sure there's enough of you?' I questioned as they led me to the Police station.

The system started once more the following day. A court hearing for breaking and entering the mobile shop; a short stay in Exeter Prison and then the long drive back to Wormwood Scrubs.

I was to wait there for re-allocation. But I had heard that the governor at Dover Borstal was a pretty good guy so I wrote asking for a second chance – and got it! Time passed smoothly as I settled back into the routine and behaved myself.

As I was driven through the gates to the railway station at Dover with my punishment behind me I couldn't help but look back up the hill at the gaunt buildings I was leaving. In some way I regretted going. It was, after all, a trouble-free life. But I was still excited about the future . . . I was just twenty and there was plenty ahead of me. What did it hold?

There was the usual anti-climax of getting out. Once back in my own area things were just the same. I stayed with Fred and Wendy in a village called Knowle, where they had a tiny flat with just a front room, bedroom and bathroom. I slept on the front room floor. Fred was working and they now had a son, Gary. I got a job as a labourer and borrowed Fred's bike to cycle to work. It wasn't long before I bumped into Bill again but even that relationship wasn't the same. A lot of the fun seemed to have gone out of life. I plodded on with the job for a month or so, getting more restless. Several times the police questioned me about jobs I hadn't done – the price of fame, I guess – and so when Bill suggested getting away I agreed. There was, of course, the old problem: money.

One night Bill turned up in a stolen car and off we went. The car broke down after a few miles so we took another and arrived in Bournemouth early the next morning. A mobile van caught our eyes and we decided to break into it, parking the car and walking back to the van. The doors were easy to force and as they creaked open what should be hanging on the back but a coat, with a wallet in the pocket. There were quite a few pounds inside so Bill grabbed it and we were loading some cigarettes into the car when a police car pulled up. On the run again! We stumbled down an alleyway in the darkness and raced up some steps into what seemed like a barn. Then we waited. As we sat among the straw Bill pulled the wallet from his pocket and shared the money out, slipping the wallet down between the wooden floor boards. For thirty minutes we waited in silence. It looked as if luck was on our side. I was just about to brush the straw off my clothes when I heard voices. Motioning Bill into silence I listened as men talked below the stairs up which we had come. There was a scratching noise. A beam of light cut through the darkness and a voice called out, 'OK – out you come!' We froze, hoping it was simply someone trying his luck. We were soon disappointed. An alsatian's head appeared at the top of the stairs.

The policemen had been down below when the wallet had slipped between the floorboards and almost hit one of them on the head!

In court there was some mix up and the magistrates were told I had no record. When I insisted I was on licence from Borstal I was accused of being a liar!

'I don't know why you decided to lie to us, Ralls. Perhaps you wanted to be big. We will give you a chance – three years on probation.'

I was staggered. Probation with my record. My jubilation didn't last long, though. As I left the court the Sidmouth police were outside and pounced on us for taking the cars. In that court there was no mistake. I was sentenced to Borstal recall so it was off to Exeter Prison to await transport.

It was becoming an all-too familiar pattern. A week or so later I was back in Wormwood Scrubs and told I would be going to Reading Borstal. This was the punishment centre for Borstal Boys in those days, a fact made clear the second I stepped into the coach in the Scrubs' yard. 'No talking,' one of the screws shouted. 'Eyes front. If your foot goes in the centre of the coach it will get stamped on. You're going to Reading and you'll learn to keep your mouths shut and jump when we say so.'

The journey passed in silence. I weighed up the future and wasn't happy. All I had heard of Reading filtered back into my mind. It was rumoured that if you were awkward the screws came into your cell at night and beat you. I didn't know if it was true – but it scared me. I consoled myself with the fact that I had survived most things so far.

I was put in a cell on my own. Any time the door was opened I had to jump to attention and give my number, name and add, 'Sir.' When the door was unlocked in the morning I had to negotiate the landing floor, polished plastic tiles which took on the consistency of glass, and carry my pot to the ablutions to empty it. When the call for breakfast came I had to run along the landing, down the spiral staircase, and then run the return journey carrying the meal with screws shouting all the time. After that it was physical training in the square and then work. And all the time the silence rule dominated. I worked in the metal recovery section, ripping bits of old equipment to pieces and separating the metal. I'd done similar work in the Scrubs.

Dinner was the same as breakfast – running, collecting and running back. Work followed. The only time we were allowed to talk was during an hour's exercise which came after the afternoon work spell; marching round in formation, arms swinging, shoulders back, for 60 minutes, chatting to anyone within earshot. We talked about anything, desperate for the opportunity to hear voices and use our own . . .

The silence of the night was occasionally broken by screams as someone snapped under the strain.

I had been planning my escape from the moment I entered Reading and asked to see the Governor as the first stage of my plan. I had, on impulse, had a swastika tattooed under the hairline of my forehead in Dover Borstal by a mate using boot polish and a needle and that was to be my secret weapon. The Governor agreed I could have the tattoo removed and I waited for the call to hospital from where I planned to run. When it came I only had two months to do which wrecked the whole plan. But I had to go through with the operation. For my treatment I was sent to Portland Borstal where it was an easier existence. I watched films and Fred and Wendy visited me. It was, in fact, the last time I would see them for years.

The day came for my operation and I was taken to the hospital, laid on a couch and given a local anaesthetic. The doctor cut the tattoo out, stitched the flaps of skin together and told me, 'That will get rid of a few wrinkles.' it was all over.

Within days I was released, but not for long. More thieving saw me with a six month sentence in prison, my first real prison sentence.

Part of it I served in Exeter, working in the mail bag shop fitting eight stitches to the inch on a never-ending stream of rough canvas mail bags.

I shared a cell with two other fellows and we amused ourselves by waving at girls in the women's prison opposite and smoking pot, smuggled in by visitors. The first time I smoked it was like a dream. I lay on the bed, sucked the cigarette and let the smoke swirl around . . . as I watched it curl upwards my mind seemed to curl with it . . . a gentle, soothing feeling. The quantity of drugs available in prison was amazing.

Because this was my first prison sentence I was moved to Haldon Camp – an open prison – and time went quickly.

On my release I decided not to return to Devon, it was dull and the constant harrassment of the police annoyed me. I decided to switch my name from Michael to Tony and try London, hoping to fool the police – with a new name. Perhaps I could find a new future. Something told me it was to be a new phase in my life. Devon was behind me. Two new friends from Haldon went with me and sketched out the London scene. It sounded inviting . . .

7: In the grip

I come from a wealthy home and had the best of education in England, France and Spain. I'm a wizard at fraud, deception etc. I earned more money than most villains before I was 20, more than most men earn in a lifetime. I was one of those cool guys who spoke well, dressed well and knew all the do's and don'ts of elite society. I was a rat and dangerous too. Well, look at me now – a lifer in Parkhurst. I was described as an extremely intelligent young man with a mind like a computer so I'm no fool. Well, I was!

J. Parkhurst Prison

The three of us arrived at Charing Cross and the lad who was a Londoner offered to watch the bags while we two went for a wash and brush up. We came out of the gents' fresh and ready to face the world and found he had gone – with our bags. 'If you can't trust a crook,' I thought bitterly! There was obviously no chance of catching him and we had no address so we were at a loss, hanging around and drinking coffee.

Around midnight we noticed a woman in her thirties eyeing us.

'Go on, give her the "come on",' said my mate.

'Not likely, she's too rough.'

'Look, idiot, we're stuck here. Somebody has got to get us into what's happening.'

I managed a weak smile and she came over. 'Are you lost, ducks? Nowhere to go?'

'You could say that.'

'Come with me. I'll get you into the scene.' And we followed her to Mick's all-night cafe in Fleet Street. I sat and looked around the crowded cafe, puzzled over the same, glazed look in each pair of eyes. It was much later that I realised they were all stoned in one way or another, drink or drugs.

I began to feel good. No dark streets like Devon. Bright lights and plenty of people. We dozed and drank in the heat of the cafe until the morning when the woman indicated we should follow her.

'You better come along to the crypt,' she explained, leading us along the street, by now bustling with newspaper vans and lorries hurrying to get news to the corners of the country. We followed across the Aldwych and along the Strand until I saw the tower of Nelson's column ahead. I watched her varicose-veined legs swing right when we got to Trafalgar Square and climb the steps of the big church there, St Martin-in-the-Fields. I didn't really see what a church could do for us but kept walking, following our guide down into the crypt: short, sturdy pillars supporting the roof and a cold brick floor. It was a sort of day centre for drug addicts and drop-outs from the West End. They were everywhere, sleeping all over the floor and filling the place with the stench of their unwashed bodies. It seemed odd to me, a church with all these tramps inside. But I was glad of somewhere to sleep so we found a corner of the floor and went to lie down.

As I dozed I had no idea that this was going to be the focal point of my existence for quite a time. I was twentyone but I hadn't the key to any door. All I had was a pitch in the corner of a church cellar.

St Martin was an appropriate saint to have given his name to the church. According to a legend he was a soldier and once riding towards a town in France, he met a beggar. Because he had no money he took his sword and sliced his cloak in half and gave half to the beggar. Lamp-posts and door handles in the area round the church have that little emblem on them.

I didn't appreciate the story for years, but I did appreciate somewhere to stay and someone to talk to. It was like a huge family, although I wouldn't trust anyone, too many of the street people were always wheeling and dealing.

I began to piece London together as well, discovering the main places. One big meeting spot was round a tea stall in Covent Garden. All the night people met. I watched for hours as they straggled around talking. Occasionally someone would wander off, to return later somehow having got money.

My money didn't last long. I survived by stealing bread and milk from the doorsteps of cafes or talking a few pence out of some of the tourists. When I was really low I existed on sauce and sugar, grabbed when I bought a cup of tea (all I could afford) from the Lyon's Corner House opposite Charing Cross Station.

All around me people were taking drugs. I remembered those joints in the prison and the way they eased my mind. Some of these people were injecting methedrine into their blood streams; some drank it down with Coke to disguise the bitter taste. I couldn't understand either way. The drinkers had ulcers cracking their mouths and some of them had both tongues and lips cracked wide open. They always seemed to be talking, gesticulating to make a point, and the pupils of their eyes were enlarged. The thought of injecting anything into my arm made me cringe. I was still a country boy finding my feet in the big city.

I spent hours chatting to the addicts, frightened of what drugs could do, but somehow drawn into their company. There was Scotch Jan, a pretty girl; Scottie, a fair-haired bloke from Glasgow; Franky girl and many others. How many are still alive I don't know . . . I shudder to think. I'd never known such a culture existed, it was all so different from the seafront at Sidmouth. Piccadilly Circus was like a homing centre for everyone, with the addicts crowding the arcades in the whole area crawling with youngsters and older down-and-outs looking for drugs, or selling them.

It didn't take me long to see how the money was to be made: women or men, sex being the currency. I copied the pattern I had observed and picked on a girl, obviously new to London. She was a Scots girl and I became her companion. She would pick up a man, take him off for a few minutes sex, and return with money. We could then go for a meal and buy methedrine or some other drug.

I convinced myself I would never fix (inject it into myself), but relentlessly the time came. I had picked up Pauline, a woman who had children. She hung around the crypt and asked me to go home with her. Pauline had a bent doctor who was giving her large prescriptions for heroin, methedrine and cocaine. One night she had a few friends in the house and the moment I was dreading arrived.

'Have a fix,' a scruffy guy said to me.

'No thanks, I can't stand needles.'

'I'll do it for you. You won't feel a thing,' he promised.

I was persuaded but looked away as they injected my arm. Whatever moment of panic I had, drifted away as soon as the drug took effect. I lay flat on my back drifting round the world.

'What an idiot I've been,' I dreamed. 'This is incredible. Fancy resisting this.' My mind wafted on . . .

I teamed up with a fellow named Freddy Robinson and we sold Pauline's drugs, taking a cut for ourselves and giving her the remainder. It was an idyllic life. I fixed more and more and because it was easy to get drugs I was soon fixing whenever I felt like it.

One day Pauline's husband appeared and Freddy and I had to disappear. That was traumatic – quick, easy drugs were not such a laugh now. One of the side effects of methedrine, combined with lack of sleep, is acute paranoia and I discovered it one day.

I rarely slept and had been awake for two or three days when suddenly it seemed everyone was after me. Men were going to blow my legs off with a shotgun. I stood in Charing Cross Road for hours holding a metal bar behind my back ready to ward off my attackers, watching the crowds of people hurrying into the station, waiting for someone to make the first move, thinking all the time they were after me. The station tannoy scared me silly; it sounded as if police messages were being broadcast for me. Taxi drivers seemed to be staring at me, in on the secret. I wandered from the station into an all-night club, sitting with my back to the wall, watching. After an hour or so I cracked completely, jumping into the centre of the dance floor shouting, 'Alright, come and get me.'

Next day I woke under a hedge, never discovering how I got there. It was the first of many times that I had the 'horrors.' Life became a blurred mixture of reality and the dreamy with an occasional trip into that frightening, nerve racking world.

I wasn't leading life any more – life was leading me!

If I wasn't waking up in the gutter, or in an unattended boiler-room below some hotel, it was a rare day. Money was now my biggest problem; not to buy food, but simply to keep my body supplied with the drugs for which it ached.

With a mate I would amble into a shop and stand near the till when there were plenty of customers around. If the assistant strayed too far I reached over the counter, grabbed a handful of notes and ran. We rarely got much and it didn't last long but it was something. For a short spell I teamed up with a male prostitute, Freddy, and it was he who tried to free me from the addiction which was now dominating my life.

We had gone into a club with a couple of Swedish girls and were sitting drinking when the 'horrors' hit me again. I dumped the girl I had picked up thinking I had been set up. I left the club and Freddy found me an hour later with my back to the wall in an underground station warning him not to come any closer. 'You're one of them,' I shouted.

He coaxed me into submission. 'Come on Tony. I'm your friend,' he soothed. 'You need to get out of London. Fancy a trip to Brighton? I hear the scene is good there and no one will follow you down there.' Somehow he got me on to a train and I slept all the way to Brighton. He booked me into a guest house and promised to return the following morning. I locked the door and fell into a sleep.

When I woke I was fresh and the fearful imaginations of the previous night had gone. Freddy was earning money but drugs were more expensive than in London and the coastline seemed dull after London's varied life.

We slept under upturned boats. One morning I woke, my clothes covered in ice, and feeling colder than I had ever felt in my life. The price of drugs gave us an idea: we agreed to return to London, buy up a load and return to sell them at the inflated Brighton prices.

It seemed a reasonable scheme so when we had saved enough from Freddy's earnings we made the trip. Returning to London's Victoria Station I patted my pocket, bulging with drugs, and contemplated the money we would make at the other end of the line. A group of men hanging around the station entrance didn't seem strange until I realised they were following us. We turned to run but they surrounded us.

'Hands against the wall,' we were ordered. I put my hands flat against the brickwork and spread my legs in the style made popular by American television films. A pair of hands frisked me, tapping the drugs expertly and finding their way into my pocket.

Fortunately Freddy hadn't been carrying any. 'He knows nothing about it,' I said, and watched as he gratefully hurried off when released.

I was taken to the police station, charged with possessing drugs, and spent a night in the cells. Being high on methedrine I couldn't sleep and the sergeant kindly gave me a pile of paper and a pencil so I spent the night drawing.

'You're going to kill yourself, son,' he said as he handed them to me. 'Why don't you get off it now, leave it alone. It's not good for you.' I nodded, thinking, 'Mind your own business. I'll not settle for a nine to five job.'

I was sent to Pentonville Prison for six months. In the first week I almost went mad as the effect of the drugs faded and my system craved more, although we were given something to help. Working in the mat shop saved me going completely berserk. With something active to do my mind was soon in gear; I would do my time and forget the outside world. Many of the faces of other prisoners were familiar. We swapped stories and each new inmate from Piccadilly would fill us in on the latest deaths.

Freddy came to visit me one afternoon and explained why the police had been waiting. Ginger Mick, an addict in Brighton, had shopped us. Freddy had got some of his mates to spread the rumour they were going to get Ginger and the addict had been so scared he had killed himself. It gave me great satisfaction.

Two places on my regular programme were the gymnasium and the church. In the gym I grew fitter as I gradually put on weight and exercised. In the church I met mates from other wings of the prison and enjoyed a laugh. It got me out of my cell.

The days dragged by. One morning I realised it was Christmas Day. I began to tot up my dismal record . . . I had been free for only one Christmas Day since my sixteenth birthday and now I was twenty-two. It was a record which didn't seem to worry me, however.

When I was released I was back to my old habits within minutes. Piccadilly drew me; some of the faces had changed but the place was the same and the circumstances were no different. All the time I was getting deeper and deeper into drugs. It was now pretty much all there was left in life.

A couple of young Americans wanted some heroin so I made up some barbiturates and crushed them into a packet telling them it was heroin. They pleaded with me and my mate to give them a fix. We did, leaving them unconscious on the floor and making sure we took their money with us.

Even friendships were turning nasty as time went on. I began to get more and more violent. Once when a man said the wrong thing to a girl I was with I freaked out completely, having to be dragged off him. I wasn't naturally violent, it was one of a few isolated incidents, but indicative of the state I was in.

Picked up by the police again I decided to ask to be cured and the courts agreed sending me to Cane Hill Hospital in South Coulsdon, Surrey.

Life there was easy to slip into. The ward into which I was put was mostly full of mental cases and it was weird. It didn't take me long to discover the drug unit and I began to get drugs off the addicts. My psychiatrist saw me occasionally and eventually I was allowed out in ordinary clothes to spend the money I got from social security. We slept in large dormitories and during the day I was able to wander round the vast grounds.

Life, of course, began to go sour. I was warned for being around the women in the hospital too much; became aggressive with the doctors and argued with one of the men in the drugs unit. It was after that argument that I put my foot in it. Called up before a doctor he gave me a puzzled look and asked, 'Don't you want to get sorted out?'

'Not really,' I replied.

My honesty floored him. 'Right, court order or not you are not staying here. You'll be put in a locked ward until we can clear it for you to go. Any trouble and you'll be back in court before you know it.' Those next few days will haunt me for the rest of my life. Locked in a ward with mental patients was either a warning or punishment, I don't know, but it was an insight into a world I had never dreamed of.

There were men who seemed intelligent but would run round exposing themselves; others would be dribbling all the time, talking to themselves or sitting on the floor for hours staring into space. I was scared. After an hour I called a nurse and pleaded, 'Look, I'm not mad like them. Let me out.' The others took up my words. 'We're not mad. Let us out.' A cruel echo of my plea. It went on for a few days and there were moments when I wondered if I was sane.

Finally with relief I was called to see a doctor and told I could go. He pointed out that I had been watched all the time; they knew everything I had been up to since arriving at the hospital; the girls and the drugs. Perhaps those final few days were deliberate . . .

Once freed, life took on its usual hue, stealing money and drugs, soliciting men for girls (pimping), mugging, and getting sicker and sicker. It seemed that nothing could help me.

A spell in Devon where I thought I could kick the drug habit showed me how wrong I was. Within weeks I was back in the West End.'

Life had fewer lighter moments. One of the rare ones occurred during a trip to Brighton with Billy Donaghue and a girl named Stephanie. Hunting for somewhere to sleep we discovered a boatyard with a nice line in yachts. Clambering aboard one of the biggest we stretched out on snow-white blanket covered bunks and slept.

I woke with Billy shaking me. 'We must be at sea,' he said.

I felt the boat sway. It was impossible. The boat had been surrounded by scaffold when we had gone aboard. We woke Stephanie and I heard voices outside. Bill decided to peep out of one of the portholes.

'You're not going to believe this – we're about thirty feet in the air of the end of a crane being lowered on to a lorry.'

Sure enough, when I looked we were. The boatyard was full of life so we sat tight, unable to leave. Before long the lorry started to rumble and we began to move. For a time we had great fun waving through the portholes at surprised people as the boat passed through towns. Eventually the driver pulled into a car park on a roadside cafe and we saw him go inside the cafe. We crept over the side and made for the road, discovering we were on the outskirts of Southampton.

Bill and I decided to make a false claim at the social security office so that we could get some cash to return to Brighton. After walking for miles to find the office and filling in the forms, using an address we'd spotted on a town map we had bought, we were shown into a waiting room. What seemed like hours later, the door opened to admit a police officer.

'When you pick an address, make sure the houses are still standing,' he laughed as we made our way to the police station, heralding another nine months in prison for me.

This time I spent my months in Winchester Prison where I passed my working hours picking vegetables. a particularly cold job in the winter.

When the sentence ended the bright lights of London beckoned me yet again. I never seemed to learn the lesson. The names had changed but the same things went on: drugs, violence and perversion and I was at the centre of it all. But things were going to change. I was facing the last few rounds of my old life if I had only known it . . .

8: Tears in the crypt

I've some news for you. I have accepted the Lord as my saviour and have peace of mind. At the moment I am serving a three year sentence and find that knowing the Good Shepherd is really a great help to me. The thing is, whether I will be able to keep it up when I am released . . .

R. Stafford Prison

Life was like a merry-go-round; sometimes the rides changed but it was gradually getting faster and I knew it was out of control. My only way out would be through death caused by drugs or in the form of a long prison term, perhaps for killing someone. It was going to be one or the other, I felt sure.

As the names and faces round me revolved I met Anita, born in the East End, Stepney and just out of Borstal. We had a funny sort of relationship, hanging round clubs at night and going our separate ways during the day. We took dope together and because Anita's veins were already riddled with needle marks I would inject into her feet occasionally, wrapping a belt round her ankle to raise the vein before spearing the needle in above her instep.

Often we'd go our own ways for weeks then team up again. I did casual work, labouring in Covent Garden or dish-washing, but preferred the old tried ways of getting money. Anita paired up with a girl named Viv, a prostitute, who was good to us both and gave us money for dope and food. It was strange really: the prostitutes were among the West End's kindest people, ready to help those like myself. Eventually Viv and Anita got a flat down the Mile End Road and I wandered back to Piccadilly for a spell.

Drugs weren't so plentiful now: many of the bent doctors had been arrested and the Government was bringing in clinics so you had to be registered to get drugs. This meant the price on the black market was creeping up. It was in Piccadilly with Viv and Anita trying to conjure up some cash for more drugs that I got into trouble again.

A guy came up to Anita and promised her a fiver if she would have sex with him. She told him to clear off but he hit her. I don't remember much of what happened except coming to with his hair in my hands. I had first kicked him in the face. He ran off.

Next day I was in Piccadilly when he re-appeared, this time with the police and I was arrested.

Now the charge was actual bodily harm although the proceedings seemed miles away as I began to twitch with the first withdrawal pangs. Life seemed a never-ending cycle of police stations, courts and prisons. This time it was Pentonville again and the old routine. As usual medication was arranged for me and after the first night or two I regained my appetite, eating as much as thirteen slices of bread in one meal just to feed my body, starved for so long. I did start to make an effort to change and went to one or two of the group meetings dealing with drugs and violence without discovering any answers. So I gave it up and concentrated on producing mats in the workroom, performing in the gym, and watching films.

Weekends were the worst. I was locked in my cell for twenty-three out of twenty-four hours. I read a lot and began to realise deep down how hooked I was. Strangely enough recognising I was an addict and institutionalised didn't seem to worry me.

I wrote a few poems to pass the time and, because a new friend, Johnny Probits from the West End, liked them, I allowed him to take them when he was released before me. He claimed he had a friend who might be able to do something with them. I didn't hear from him but on my release I found my way back to the crypt at St Martins, remembering he had been writing to someone there. I asked for the man I had seen him address his letters to, Norman Ingram-Smith, and was taken to a waiting room packed with alcoholics and addicts. I almost ran. A woman came to the door and called my name, I followed her into a small room and saw a man wearing glasses behind a desk.

I'd taken about six ampoules of physepton before plucking up courage to go to the crypt so I was pretty high, and couldn't remember much of what he said.

I began to act strangely. I asked where Johnny was and then burst into tears. The tears just flowed and I couldn't stop. I thought it was the drugs but more likely it was the years of frustration piling up and breaking out. It was my first contact with a Christian.

'Sorry about that,' I muttered when it was over, and made a dive for the door.

'Come again,' he said. 'Tears can wash away a lot. Don't be ashamed.'

As I reached for the door he added: 'I'll be here if you need me again. I'll make an appointment for you tomorrow morning at nine thirty. Alright?'

'Sure,' I said, not meaning to come anywhere near the crypt next day.

'Would you like some money?'

'No, it's OK,' I said although what made me refuse I don't know, my meagre prison allowance had been spent within minutes of my release on drugs. I made my way out and shuffled back through the crowded but lonely streets to Piccadilly.

Anita and Viv were around the clubs so I spent the night with them, wandering half-frozen, dirty and tired round the West End. One-legged Tommy was around, one of the usual crowd, and he took me into a toilet for a fix. He was an artist who would draw for anyone who asked.

As I drifted along under the influence of the drugs I realised it was almost nine o'clock in the morning and remembered the provisional date with Norman. 'I might as well go,' I told myself. 'It's a free cup of tea.'

I carefully avoided the issue when Norman raised the subject of me coming off drugs as we talked. I liked the guy – he was direct and honest and seemed to want to help.

I was given a flat, owned by the unit, to live in but was asked to leave after smuggling a girl into my room. Then Norman offered to let me sleep in the waiting room, which became my bedroom for the next three months. He then arranged for me to go to a clinic, St Bernards, to be cured. I was put to bed for days, sleeping mostly but being woken occasionally to be given pills. My dreams were vivid with colours I had never seen before and they continued until the treatment was over and I was up and about walking in pyjamas and dressing gown. I'd like to say I felt better, but all I got was itchy feet. Late one night I gave up, asked for my clothes, and headed for the old haunts.

The cure didn't last long. I ended it in the toilets at Piccadilly Circus having a fix and soon I was back into everything.

I met Johnny, who had lost the book of poems, and visited Norman occasionally, sensing his disappointment at my failure but not being able to understand why he didn't lecture me.

With Norman's encouragement I tried another clinic in a Church Army hostel in Great Peter Street, lasting only a few days before drifting away. The old life pulled too hard.

By now I was getting drugs prescribed legally which made it easier to score. Even a holiday in Cornwall at a farm didn't work; I left after a while and found my way back to London. So relieved was I to get back that I made straight for Piccadilly and snatched the first drugs available, barbiturates. I sat down to have a fix and then, nothing . . . total blackout.

When I came to, hours later, I was in St Martins' social unit. 'You walked in with a syringe hanging out of your arm,' I was told. I was really worried; I'd heard about barbiturate blackouts and it seemed everything was happening to me. Apparently I had fallen over and the syringe had gone into a nerve. I had to use a metal support on my wrist for months and do exercises to regain the strength and proper use of the arm.

I agreed to give Cornwall another try, but still it didn't work out and the Bibles lying around the place didn't mean anything to me. I returned to London after getting high, overdoing the fun, and swearing at the receptionist at a local doctor's surgery.

The Chelsea clinic made another attempt to dry me out and it seemed to work. I was cured enough to help put on a sort of drama show, enacting the life of an addict. Professional actors came to help us as it was a fund raising effort. I recall Judy Geeson and Sheila Hancock were among those I met.

I was living in a hostel run from St Martins and even though I didn't go home on a number of evenings they didn't seem perturbed.

Then I met Christine. Most of the girls I knew were prostitutes, but Christine was completely different. Smart, clean, bright and a Christian, she spent hours talking to me at the centre. She tried to persuade me to go to a Christian centre she knew of. I wasn't interested. Mick and Rosie, a couple I had met in Cornwall, had gone to work at the centre which was run by a fellow called Frank, she explained.

'You ought to give it a chance,' she pleaded. I still wasn't interested.

'You can't go on like this,' she insisted. 'You need a new life.'

I wandered off. It seemed there was no hope of a fresh start. I was trapped. I had run out of places to go. Everywhere I went turned out to be the same: drugs, mugging, fighting and arguing. And I was heading for prison again . . . for the last time.

I was wandering along one day when I spotted two of the girls from the clinic in Chelsea. They were being shouted at by a man and as I watched he started to push them around. Something snapped inside me. I vaulted a railing, chased across the road and jumped him.

Later that day the police took me. I pleaded guilty; there was no point in not doing so. I knew the magistrates would listen to the smart guy who I had beaten up.

Six months. Pentonville Prison. What was new?

What was new was that something was happening inside me. Lying on the bunk one evening I started to think. I was coming up to twentyfive and my whole life was one long cycle of drugs, violence and prison. I had tried everything I knew but couldn't break the cycle. That night I realised that there was no hope.

In between my regular blackouts, bouts of paranoia, and overdoses, I knew I wouldn't last much longer. Many of the people I had known had died. In my bottom bunk I stared at the base of the bed above me . . . a water pump throbbed throughout the night outside the window . . . my two companions snored noisily . . . what a life!

Then came the letter. Christine wrote explaining again about the Christian community somewhere in the wilds where there was a chance for me. She asked if I would like to see the guy who ran the place.

'No way,' I thought. But then, realising the desperate plight

I was in, something impelled me to write back and agree to the meeting. Frank Wilson and another man, Tony, himself an ex-addict, came to see me some weeks later. 'We won't ram Christianity down your throat,' they promised. 'We have a place if you want it. You are very welcome.'

Tony told me about how he had been on drugs and how Jesus had cured him. 'He can cure you, too,' he promised, his eyes rivetting me with the message. Cynically I thought, 'You've got to say that; your boss is here.' But I gave him a hearing as I rolled a fag.

'Right,' I said suddenly sitting up and coming to a decision. 'I'll take your word and come. But I don't want to know about religion – I can get myself off without that.'

'Fair enough,' Frank promised. 'Drop me a line and tell me when you are leaving and we'll make the arrangements.'

That day I explained my intentions to a fellow prisoner, Danny, as we walked round the exercise yard. Irish Danny was from the Piccadilly scene and understood my dilemma. He wished me luck, adding, 'I don't know anyone who has really got off.' We talked about religion, both being Roman Catholics, and agreed that if there was anything to confess a death-bed confession was good enough. Death didn't frighten me . . . in many ways it would have been a welcome relief.

I wrote to Frank and gave him a release date, actually giving him a date just after my real release. I wanted some time to have a last fling.'

The date drew near and something impelled me to write again, giving the correct date. Later I found a youth group in a church had been praying for me. I also wrote to Norman and told him what was happening. He invited me to breakfast on the day of my release, one way of making sure he could get me on the train to the centre.

My final night in prison arrived. I was alone with my letters as company: one from Christine and one from Frank. I knew it would be my last chance. I couldn't cheat death much longer if I continued the way I was. I didn't know what I feared most, the thought of continuing to live pumped full of drugs and violence, or the possibility of life free from all that which posed an even bigger mystery. Time would tell.

9: A whole new life

You said, when you came here, about Jesus coming into your life. You may think this stupid but what did it feel like? Can you explain how one minute you were like me, and the next you're clean? Now you are clean and going straight do you ever get feelings of looking back? Do you get into trouble, or have policemen coming to your door?

E. Pucklechurch Remand Centre

Norman greeted me like a long lost friend when I made my dazed way into St Martins, still feeling the effect of the fix I had taken. I was getting higher and higher.

He knew, and so did Ruth, a social worker who sat me down and pottered around getting breakfast. St Martins was almost like home to me. A feeling of fondness came over me as I looked around the familiar setting. Inside me a battle was raging, 'Why go away? What good will it do? You've tried it all before.'

They must have known what was going on because the pair of them gently, but firmly, made certain I reached the station and refused to leave until I was safely settled in a corner seat. They waited on the platform until the train pulled out. Another stage in my life was beginning.

By the time the train reached its destination I was fighting the full effects of the drugs from the morning. Somehow I made it from the carriage and spotted Mike, whom I remembered from Cornwall, coming towards me. He put his arms round me, hugged me, and led me to a car.

I dozed as the car twisted its way through the country lanes. Some hidden sense made me rouse and look up as we approached a sign carrying the drawing of a boat . . . Mike clicked the indicator and we turned left into a long tree-lined drive. Through the trees a house appeared, a large rambling mansion, The New Life for the World Centre.

We drove by the front of the building and into a courtyard, surrounded on three sides by parts of the mansion. Mike helped me out and urged me towards a door in the centre section. It was near the dining room and as I looked, I saw Rosie's cheerful face peeping through a hatch.

'Hello Tony,' she called.

Others were sitting round the dining room in groups, chatting and looking comfortable. I couldn't eat, though. Instead I was taken to a room and without even looking round I sat in a chair and fell asleep for the afternoon.

It was easy getting into the routine of the place. After all I'd been through one place was much the same as another. True the daily events were different here; there was chapel in the morning, then breakfast followed by cleaning duties which we all shared. During the afternoon various other jobs around the house and garden were allocated to me and in the evening the meal was followed by more activities. At first it was irksome: I felt I needed more than the one free evening I was allowed each week. Later I came to realise that too much free time would have led many to drift away through sheer boredom.

The house itself was impressive. Fifty-seven rooms ranging from enormous barn-size lounges (some in disrepair) to small bedrooms. A huge central staircase twisted upwards from the large hall. Outside the grounds stretched away and included ornamental lakes, some of which were overgrown. The courtyard was surrounded by what had probably once been stables but were now comfortable rooms and a dining area. The countryside round the house was beautiful, with the nearest village, Blockley, about a mile away. It was very different from the West End.

I asked for, and got, a tough manual job digging trenches for pipes and Frank agreed that I could work in the evenings instead of going to chapel and the various Christian activities which were put on. I was determined to keep clear of the Christian bit and prove I could break from drugs on my own. The Sunday services were a bore and often I walked out in the middle. When they sang hymns I found myself looking round at the others.

The days turned into weeks and the weeks into the first month. I watched and picked fault with anything I could. All the time I saw others coming to the centre and becoming Christians but I was determined not to let crack the protective shell I had built around myself.

Every so often someone would chat to me about 'the Lord' but their words meant nothing. I palled up with a new guy called Brian only to find that within a short time he became a Christian. 'Perhaps God doesn't want me,' I joked.

Despite my reluctance I was beginning to see that something was making a difference to the others. My talks with addicts reminded me about the drug scene and the craving returned but by now I was realistic and sane enough to know that it was no use.

After two or three months the constant pressure of services, talking and seeing lives changed, began to get to me. Frank sat talking with me for a whole evening; I desperately wanted to believe but couldn't. I was prayed for many times but somehow it didn't seem to work.

Something, however, had to give. I was torn between the possibilities of a new life and the problems of the old. Late one night I turned to God in desperation, realising that it was either back to the West End or into the new life I had seen springing up all around me. 'God, if you are real come into my life and help me,' I cried. And suddenly a peace came over me as if my past no longer mattered.

I saw no vision but felt a presence I couldn't understand: there was no-one with me, I was alone. Somehow I knew I had made contact with Jesus.

It was true, he could change me. The date stuck in my mind, November 22nd, 1970, a date carved on my memory.

I didn't want to admit this change, though. After kicking up such a fuss for so long I had to find the courage to tell Rosie. She hugged me and welcomed me to the family, promptly announcing the news to everyone within earshot. Sheepishly I had to keep admitting the change as workers and addicts came to me asking, 'Is it true?'

I found myself singing hymns, flung myself into all the activities that were going on, and started to read my Bible and pray with enthusiasm. Many of the words in the Bible were foreign to me but I grasped the truth that mattered: Jesus loved me, had died for me. He was answering my prayers. On some days it was almost like being on drugs, I was high with the excitement of it all. Gradually, however, it began to fade; Bible reading became hard and prayer times tough. I couldn't understand it. I had expected things to be different and easy. My friend Brian was experiencing similar problems and we talked about it. He had a wife and child and was being drawn back to the old scene. The day he went I walked down the drive with him trying vainly to make him stay. As he waved goodbye I shouted into the heaven, 'Why are you letting him go if you're so great? Why don't you stop him?' I got no answer but felt better for it.

The pressure mounted. One day I was painting some woodwork in the house when suddenly I felt fed up. I put the brush down and walked off to get changed. I was going back. A few people tried to talk me out of it but I refused. One of the staff, Peter Ward, dropped me off at the station and I sat on the platform waiting for the train. The delay brought the dream to an end. 'What am I doing?' I asked myself. I phoned the centre and was taken back.

I knew I was a Christian but couldn't understand why I wasn't drastically different. A guy ribbed me during a meal-time and I flipped a cup of hot tea into his face. Another day I tried to push someone over the bannister when I lost my temper. Mick, Rosie's husband, broke it up. It was as though a battle was raging inside me: I knew the Lord, yet wanted life on my terms. I began to realise that though I had become a Christian it didn't suddenly mean I was a different person. I was a new creature (2 Corinthians 5:17) sure enough, but it was up to me to allow the Holy Spirit to change my violent nature. Knowing that, and doing something about it, were different things. I knew it would be tough. My weak-willed past began to grip me until one day I just walked out, went to the station, and boarded the first train to London.

I had heard about the Holy Spirit giving people power to conquer old habits; I knew I needed power in my life; but I was tired of trying. I was on my way back to the West End. It looked as if the drugs had beaten the new life. Even Jesus wasn't strong enough.

10: Slipping and conquering

When I was a child whenever I had to go to the doctor or dentist my mum went with me. She never said I would not have pain but that I must be brave and strong. Holding her hand gave me courage. It is the same with God. He never promised we would not have pain in our lives but holding his hand gives me courage.

A. Dartmoor Prison

I hit the West End later that evening and soon scored. But somehow as I stretched on a park bench after the injection, it wasn't as it had been on previous occasions. Wandering round the clubs was strange, as if I was looking down on myself and disapproving. I didn't fit any more. I was an outsider. For two days and nights I tried to recapture the carefree spirit I had once shown . . . it wouldn't come. No amount of drugs could excite me.

It didn't take much thinking to realise what was wrong: I was missing the Christians who had become my friends. Rosie's cheerful face, Frank's personality, Mick's concern . . .

I made my way to a telephone kiosk and dialled the number.

'Can I speak to Frank,' I asked when I heard the number. As his voice came from through the line I posed another question: 'Frank, it's me, Tony. Can I come back?'

He must have heard my sigh of relief when he agreed.

Even in the tranquil surroundings of Northwick Park, the Life for the World Centre, I couldn't ignore the struggle going on inside me. The tension was at its greatest when I linked up with a girl who was there from the drug scene. When chapel was on in the evenings we would ignore the meeting and meet by the stables. All the while I lay there with her I knew that not only was it wrong but that I couldn't keep up the double life I was leading much longer.

As I went back to my room after the second night with her I felt grubby. The battle raged on more than one front. I was smoking heavily, despite a no smoking rule having been introduced. Most of the guys had agreed and decided it was a good thing. I didn't disagree, though I was concerned for those smokers who might not come to the centre because of the rule and could miss everything else on offer. My sexual problems and the cigarettes were like two giant beasts towering above me, too huge to conquer and yet if I was to mean business with God I knew I must beat them.

That evening in the cool isolation of my bedroom I puzzled over the problem facing me. Drugs and institutions had stamped their marks, leaving deep wounds of immaturity which didn't seem to heal. The weak will which had led me into a lifetime of trouble was unable to combat elements I felt I ought to conquer if I were to live a victorious life. On the one hand Jesus Christ was very real to me and I knew convincingly that I was a Christian; on the other hand I continually stumbled over so many habits and weaknesses that I couldn't imagine myself as a useful member of any church. My weakness showed itself when Leslie appeared at the centre. Like me he couldn't beat the old habits. He told me he had a couple of hundred pounds and invited me to take him to London to 'show him the scene.' A Coventry lad, it was his third time at Northwick Park.

The first stop after leaving the centre was in the village shop where I bought a packet of fags. By the time the train arrived in London we had smoked the lot. I made for the East End where I knew Anita and Viv lived and, using Leslie's money, we bought drugs. In the house we fixed Leslie and watched him flake out straight away on the floor. I roared with laughter realising that for all his brave talk he hadn't been used to taking many fixes. I fixed myself and sat round chatting to the girls.

During the train journey Leslie had explained that he hadn't all his money with him, he would have to wait until Life for the World sent it on. That seemed reasonable since they often looked after people's money and usually refused to allow folk to take it with them when they left, preferring to send it to a proper address later.

The girls agreed to let us stay until the money came through. It took a day or so to realise that the money wasn't going to come; Leslie had been fantasising. Anita and Viv agreed to let us stay one more night, asking us to be on the move the next day.

That night I slept on the couch. I had bought some stuff from Viv the night before and used half, leaving the remainder in its container in an egg cup on the mantlepiece for use next morning. During the night I sensed someone was in the room, and squinting through half-open eyes saw Viv carefully pour the drug into another container and tip water into the ampoule. I didn't say anything, feeling cold and totally lost. The only friends I had were turning me over.

The only friends I had . . . those words hit me hard. These girls weren't my friends. My friends were back at Life for the World; Frank and the others who loved me whatever I did. I messed them around and still they cared. And God cared for me through them. Those workers at Northwick Park could have been earning a good living in ordinary jobs, they all had qualifications, but they had given it up to help others like me. Rosie and Mick had never had their own home . . . because of me and people like me.

I left next morning with Leslie. Feeling like a fish that had been hooked out of the water, floundering about on the bank, I felt I couldn't ring Frank again; this time I had gone too far. Leslie, however, decided he wanted to go back so I took him to a phone box and waited outside while he made his call. He chatted away, occasionally glancing through the small square windows in my direction before pushing open the door and leaning out. 'Frank wants a word.'

I squeezed past and picked up the phone. 'You are welcome to come back if you want to,' said a voice at the other end.

'Why me?' I blurted out.

'Because God loves you and has things planned for you,' he replied.

I was stunned. They still cared.

'Okay,' I said, the decision made.

I walked with fresh vigour through the crowded streets with Leslie trailing at my heels until I came to St Martins. Norman, always faithful Norman, arranged a travel warrant for us and before long we were on the train.

Mick picked us up at the station and I must admit I was very subdued. But it was incredible, I was made so welcome, no one talked to me as if I had done wrong. It seemed as if I could slip right back into gear again.

That night Frank tapped on my door and entered. I had taken my shirt off and he pointed his finger at the needle marks tracking my arm. 'This is it,' he warned. 'You have a lot going for you and God is going to use you.' I felt stupid and close to tears mumbling a sort of thank-you.

But next day the old battles returned. I cycled to the pub in the evening and bought some cigarettes. It was wrong; it was against the rules; but what could I do? I hadn't the will power to resist.

One day Frank called me into his office. I faced him across the table strewn with papers, paper clips and pens.

'Tony, this is it. You have to decide. Is it to be Christ, or your own life? I must tell you this, that unless you decide soon the decision will be made for you.'

That heralded a fresh bout of internal struggling. I knew I could cut myself off from God or really go on with Him. I wanted to go on so badly but could I do it? I forced myself to endure the chapel services and gradually began to sense God speaking to me. In the past I felt that all the leaders had got together with whoever was speaking and given him a few pointers about some of the things I had been doing so that they could fit them into the sermon. Now I began to realise it wasn't like that – it was simply that God wanted to talk to me personally and was using other people as His voice.

One Sunday evening the service had followed its normal free and easy pattern. We'd sung hymns and choruses, prayed and praised and some of the people there had talked about their needs. Then Frank spoke, flipping through his Bible with every verse hitting me hard. I knew it was God working on me again. As Frank finished I breathed a sigh of relief . . . almost over, I thought.

Then Frank did something he rarely did, he looked over the small congregation and said, 'Is there anyone here who wants to get right with God and be filled with the Holy Spirit?'

My heart thumped with a fresh turmoil. I knew I had to get right soon, time was running out, but to do it in front of all these people, that was something different. Tony Ralls, the braggart, the one who talked so boldly about the dope scene, the one who ridiculed everything in sight . . . I couldn't do it.

I felt a stirring inside, a physical feeling which made me stand, rush forward and kneel at the front of the chapel with my head on the table. I confessed everything I could think of, not pausing for breath, and suddenly there was peace. Great gulps of peace like drinking water.

I realised that others were kneeling alongside me and Frank was moving slowly along the line praying personally with each individual. He stood by me and put his hands on my head praying that the Holy Spirit would baptise me to overflowing.

Tears were in my eyes and with them I felt the muck of my previous life was being washed away.

In a low voice Frank spoke, 'You have been filled with the Spirit.'

I didn't feel any different but I knew something had happened. Rosie and others crowded up, flinging their arms round me as I went from person to person apologising for some of the things I had done and said.

I knelt by my bed later that evening to pray and found myself speaking in a language I didn't understand . . . it seemed that a tap had been turned on inside me and new life and new love came flowing out. At last I was looking down on my problems instead of being bowed down by them.

I knew it was a key experience, a turning point in my Christian life. The battles ahead wouldn't be any smaller or any less fierce but somehow I knew I could face them. I now had the capacity to draw on spiritual weapons for the spiritual warfare I was to be involved in.

It wasn't easy. Some nights after that incredible experience of being filled with the Holy Spirit I found myself cycling to the pub again in the evenings . . . except that now something gave me the strength to turn the bike in the road and head back to the centre. The impulse to return to the West End seemed to disappear too. Life was taking on a more positive view.

There were still problems. Sleep was one of the major ones. Like many ex-addicts I found I couldn't rest at nights and only managed to sleep the night through about once every week or so because of the regular routine and the lack of drugs in my system. I turned that to my advantage by praying in those sleepness nights – I lay praying in tongues and gradually natural, healthy long hours of sleep became normal. Masturbation was another problem I knew I had to conquer and even though it didn't totally go until the day I got married six years later I knew long spells of victory and was at peace.

My dream life was chaotic with erotic and violent dreams. At first it was a tremendous stumbling block until I began to realise that the input into my subconscious over the years had to come out somewhere – I likened it to a blocked drain. As clean water is forced through and the drain is rodded the muck begins to flow away. It was like that with me. After twenty-five years of my sort of life style, I needed long-term cleansing treatment.

I continued to be critical of others and had to learn to control my tongue, discovering the discipline of my previous boxing training helped. I had learned to lead with my left hand and, like any youngster, had found it awkward. After much practice it became natural. As I realised just how critical I was I began to make the same sort of effort to control myself and it worked, though sometimes I dropped my guard and caught one on my chin.

I needed control in other areas. It seemed I was always saying sorry, but I knew that Jesus understood.

Many young Christians are given the impression that immediately they make that decision their lives are changed and all old attitudes disappear overnight. I've not found it to be true. Young Christians need to realise that they have to learn a new way of life – and much of it is hard graft, and sheer willpower which, with the help of the Holy Spirit, gets easier.

I had a hunger for prayer and reading my Bible. Tony Copeland and I were given permission to study in the afternoon and I found myself reading the Bible at every opportunity. I started a Bible correspondence course and seemed to devour books like Watchman Nee's The Normal Christian Life, and books by Torrey, Andrew Murray and other well-known Christian authors.

One of my major difficulties was depression which could hit me at the most unlikely times so that I sat for hours in my room staring at the wall. It was like a big cloud coming between me and the sun but as my relationship with Jesus grew so the sun shone more often and the cloud drifted away.

In practical terms my life changed also. I went to all the meetings and began to go out a lot to give my testimony at various rallies in churches and halls, enjoying witnessing to God's transforming power.

Of course that led to moments of jealousy among the ex-addicts in the community but it showed me that we were like children and needed to grow more in the things of God.

Tony and I spent hours painting to restore old rooms in the mansion to bring them back into use and as the rooms were opened I began to feel useful.

I was hit by conflicting emotions. I wanted to be the centre of attraction but yet didn't want to be. After years of being the centre of activity with police, social services, probation officers, welfare officers, psychologists and so on, I found it hard to adjust to the fact that Jesus was now beginning to ask me to shoulder responsibilities and grow up.

There was to be a big meeting in the Dome at Brighton with Roger and Jan, a singing team, leading and others sharing in the ministry. I was with a group who were sent on ahead to spread the news. I lodged in a Christian home and toured local churches giving my testimony with Tony. We became known as the Two-Tone team . . . we were always together. After the meeting in the Dome other appearances followed – including taking part in crusades run by the late Dr Eric Hutchings in Hastings and Bournemouth.

It was during these meetings when I became aware of the tensions beforehand, and when girls began to ask me for my autograph when I had spoken I began to be cynical; another problem I had to fight.

I continued to study, pray and read my Bible and was growing in God despite all the tensions within. Which in fact helped me; I began to face up to life as it was.

In the course of the next month or so I had to pass through the West End a few times and, although I still felt a pull, it was getting much weaker. I knew then that it would go completely.

Tony was a great help; we prayed together a lot. I felt my testimony was being used in the various meetings and on one occasion suddenly felt the urge to speak in tongues out loud. I realised the dangers but felt so sincerely that God wanted this, that I did it. My heart thumped as I completed the message and sat down, knowing how unbiblical it was without an interpretation. Suddenly someone stood and gave the meaning. Joy flooded into me. Afterwards another person came up to me and quietly said the message was specifically for him . . . it was a great encouragement.

The meetings at Northwick Park were a seed-bed for encouraging me in corporate worship – and yet allowing my individuality. Tony and I were invited to take meetings in the chapel and grew. I realised it was important for former addicts such as myself to be filled with the Holy Spirit because of the strength He gave me to withstand the pressures and pulls of the old life.

In my raw enthusiasm I returned to the clinic where I had made a vain attempt to dry-off a year or so earlier and spoke to the patients about my faith. On reflection I probably rammed my beliefs down their throats. I trust God to forgive such impetuous behaviour.

I chatted with Frank about leaving the centre. He felt I should stick it out a bit longer but as I felt ready to move on he promised to look out for an opening for me. While waiting I went on another series of meetings, this time with the blind pianist Peter Jackson. It was thrilling to see the way God was blessing him and I realised just how God could use me if I surrendered everything to him.

I knew then that I could stand outside Northwick Park: I knew I could stand even in London. Those beliefs were soon to be put to the test.

Frank called me into his office. 'You've been here eight months, Tony,' he said. I looked round the old familiar room; it seemed a lot longer, a whole life-time, in fact, since I had first arrived.

'I have a job for you if you want to leave,' he went on.

I jumped at the chance. 'Sure Frank, what is it?'

'It is in the film library run by the Billy Graham Association.'

'That sounds marvellous,' I enthused. 'Where?'

'In London.' I was silent.

'Do you think you can handle it?' he asked.

'I'm certain,' I replied looking him in the eyes.

After an interview I was accepted. A few days later I packed my few belongings into a couple of holdalls, stuffed my Bible on the top, and closed the door to my room at Northwick for the last time. Rosie put her arms round me. 'We'll miss you, Tony,' she said. 'But God is going to use you – you see.'

I was taken to the station and leaned back into the seat as the train rocked along a now familiar route. I was going back to London. But this time I was a Christian going to a Christian job and stepping into a new future. There was a strange mixture of fear and bubbling excitement. It was one thing to be a Christian in the middle of the country with nice people but would I be able to cope in London among the temptations which had beaten me before? The only thing I was certain of was that Jesus would support me.

11: The Amsterdam affair

I'm doing four years for robbery and burglary and am pleased to say all I have left to do is three months. Before I was nicked I was heavily addicted to speed pills and at one time was taking about seventy to one hundred pills a day. It is only prison that has saved me from an early grave. Drugs have ruined my life but I don't know if I will be able to resist the temptation when I get out.

K. Camphill Prison, near Newport, Isle of Wight.

I went to a house in Goodwin Road, Forest Gate, in South London, an ordinary terraced house which had been given to the Life for the World to use. A guy called Graham was there, a young Christian who was training to be a lawyer, and the brother of Christine, the girl who had first spoken to me when I was in the clinic in Chelsea. For the first time in many years I was leading my own life. At twenty-six, I was having my first taste of adult life. The house was a typical bachelor pad, disorganised and with the kitchen constantly piled with used saucepans as we experimented at cooking.

On the following Monday I started work. I caught a train into Liverpool Street and then took the Underground, travelling on the Central Line until I needed to change to the Northern Line for Camden Town. I was so full of joy with the new life that I found myself smiling and wishing everyone 'good morning'. Many thought I was a bit nutty. I also developed a technique for Bible study . . . I read parts of the New Testament into central London, and the Old Testament on the way out during the return trip in the evening. That forty-five minute journey was an adventurous time. Jesus was becoming a close and valuable friend. I got up early to pray and study the Bible; I was keen to face up to the challenge of living for Him.

My job was interesting and varied. The Billy Graham office was on the second floor of a modern office block, a large semi-open plan office with a few smaller offices spattered round the side. My work was mainly checking the many Billy Graham films when they were returned from showings in various halls and churches. If they were broken, and sometimes they were, I mended them. I also had to make sure that films were sent to their different venues in time for the showing. In some ways that was exciting; I knew they would be used to help people. Sometimes I would check a lot of films, spending the whole afternoon watching Billy Graham preach at crusades all over the world. It was tremendously good for my Christian education.

The people I worked with were marvellous company, Christians from all walks of life. They loved Jesus and followed Him. I was so enthusiastic I found myself constantly praising the Lord, often slipping into tongues. I had a roof over my head, a job, friends and most of all Jesus Christ had given me a new life.

Graham, from the house I lived in, made sure I met other Christians. One day he took me to meet a group of young people in South Croydon. As I talked to them about my past and the dramatic change in my life I felt a freedom and excitement that was somehow special. The meeting was in the home of a woman named Joy who had lost her husband tragically and had brought up three sons. She radiated love. We began to talk after the meeting and I discovered something about the group; a link in the chain of my life that we didn't realise was there.

I recalled my last few weeks in Pentonville Prison and the time I wrote to Frank Wilson giving him a false release date. Suddenly I had changed my mind and written to him giving the correct date. I discovered it was this group of young people who had been praying for me, thanks to Christine. As we all realised just how my life had hung in the balance and their prayers had incredibly brought about the change in direction we praised the Lord and laughed together – it was some night!

They were part of a whole new range of friends I developed within months of leaving Northwick Park. Most evenings I was invited out to eat somewhere. But churches were something different. I found the traditional forms of worship hard to handle and began to realise just how few people believed in the baptism in the Holy Spirit in the same way that I did. I found myself growing confused and then arrogant, arguing about the different forms of church life with Graham and others. Sensitivity came hard, but it came slowly.

I heard of a coffee bar based at All Souls Church in Langham Place, at the top of Oxford Street, from nine o'clock on Friday nights until six thirty the following morning and decided to go along and use it as a base to reach my old contacts in the West End.

We gathered for prayer at the start of the evening and then split up to wander round the city inviting people back for soup and to talk about the Lord. The first night I slipped off on my own and made my way back to my old haunts. I took a handful of gospel leaflets, but it proved to be tough going.

People I had been close to in the past didn't want to know me now. When I last saw her, Frankie was good looking: when I met her that evening she was ravaged by drugs and her life as a prostitute. I found it difficult to talk to her so I muttered something and gave her a couple of pounds.

When I got home, tired and worn out on Saturday morning, I wept inside as I thought of the old friends I had met and the way their lives were trickling away. I desperately wanted them to come to Jesus, but knew most of them wouldn't. I began to operate in Piccadilly Circus again.

'I thought I'd heard you'd gone religious,' said Danny, one of the men I had spent time with in Pentonville. He staggered on, drugged to the eyeballs, unimpressed by my words. Then I almost bumped into Mugsy; we had six months together inside. He was stoned and had his arm in a sling. 'I am not in need,' he blubbered and my heart went out to him . . . he didn't really know what he needed, but I did. Dirty and looking ill he'd only been out three weeks and was tough and hard inside.

My faith became more real and stronger as I spent time in the West End, sometimes with other Christians, sometimes alone. As I reached Piccadilly one night I saw a crowd in the middle of the Circus. A gang of men were beating someone up; bystanders were just watching. Full of fear I went across not knowing what to do. I called out, 'The police are coming,' apologising to the Lord under my breath for the lie. As they heard me they turned and ran. God was on my side! Even the guy they had been beating ran, pressing his hands to a bleeding face.

He looked at me with fear in his eyes, perhaps thinking I was one of them. I couldn't understand why the people standing round had done nothing.

Occasionally some of the down-and-outs I met and prayed with turned to Christ. One night someone asked me to pray for him in a cinema queue when I was giving out literature. It was amazing what God was able to do.

My work with the Billy Graham organisation was going well and occasionally I would spend a weekend at Northwick Park, a living testimony to what God could do, in an effort to encourage some of the new people there.

Occasionally God did show me very sharply that I wasn't perfect, and it hurt. One of the most painful lessons was when I was tramping the streets of London wanting to share my faith with anyone.

One night I met Viv, another link with the past, and talked with her about the Lord. My words fell on deaf ears. A couple of times I met her and talked but each time she was unimpressed.

I thought that if I took her out for a meal we would have more time and things could develop more naturally. They did. I ended up in bed with her! It was a tremendous jolt to realise what I had done. I knew that if I was a Christian I shouldn't do such things and yet found myself unable to cope with my desires. I learned what Paul meant in Romans 7, 'What I want to do I do not do, but what I hate I do.' (NIV).

I was learning that the devil was real, and alive, and actively trying to trip me up. True it was my own desire that had caused me to fall but the thought of the evil one gloating made me shiver. I wanted to give up this whole Christian thing. I had let God down so badly. 'Steady on,' a wiser Christian friend counselled me when I confessed to him. 'It's not the end of the world. The devil's probably found he can't get you back on the drugs so he's trying something else. You can't afford to slip in any area.'

Romans 8 then became very real to me, 'There is now no condemnation for those who are in Christ Jesus . . . ' (NIV). I learnt that as long as I really repented God would continue to help me. I realised then why so many of my friends went out in pairs, it was a sensible precaution. I needed to be careful in every aspect of my life. Encouraged by sensible Christians and some Bible verses which spoke very strongly to me I determined not to fall again . . . I would, but I eventually learned.

Back at Northwick Park a film was to be made of the work there and I was asked if I would be in it. I agreed, realising just how useful it could be to people on drugs to see the power of God to help them. I linked with Jimmy Swalkhammer, the producer, who himself had been through a tough time before becoming a Christian.

I was to stand in Piccadilly Circus and talk into the camera about what God had done for me. It was a strange experience standing there with people all around going about their own business, and yet talking about Jesus. As the cameras stopped rolling and the team disappeared I was left alone in the Circus and suddenly felt depressed. I was assaulted by a tremendous urge to go back to drugs. Somehow I managed to pray and as I did so strength seeped into my spirit and I became stronger.

It was, however, indicative of the tremendous struggles in the life of young Christians, struggles emphasised even more in those from difficult backgrounds such as myself. The knowledge of my own temptations and hard times was to be an invaluable aid in helping others in years to come.

Life went on, packed with witnessing, meeting friends, and riding the motor bike I had now bought myself. Then Frank Wilson contacted me again. He wanted me to go with him to Amsterdam, Holland, to take part in a Congress of Evangelism arranged by the Billy Graham Organisation. Two thousand evangelists were to be there and he wanted me to give my testimony one evening explaining how Jesus had taken me off drugs.

My companion on the trip was to be Tony Copeland from Northwick Park. I was delighted because although I had kept in touch, and even visited his parents in Wisbech, he was slipping away and finding the tug of the old life too hard at the time.

I knew how he felt. The times I kept slipping were constant reminders of how strong the past was. And the pressure was growing. I found it strange that people who refused to give me a fix when I was a drug addict were offering me free drugs now I was a Christian.

The weeks before the congress slipped by. In the Billy Graham office we had speakers to take the midweek meeting. Once the Jesus People came. I had heard a lot about them from television and what was happening in America. I copied what they did, particularly fixing Jesus stickers everywhere until I realised what a lot of work I was causing for the people who had to remove them. I spent time with the Jesus People and was invited for an afternoon at their flat by their leader, Faith. They told me I should give up all my possessions . . . that it wasn't right to work . . . I should cut myself off from everyone I knew . . . 'You are not of this world,' they warned me. 'Praise the Lord,' was constantly on their lips but as the afternoon wore on it didn't seem to ring true. I asked why they were dressed in the shabby way they were, very much as I was when I was on the dope scene. My questions proved too much. 'If you don't want to become a real disciple fair enough. Come back if you want to,' Faith told me as I was shown the door.

I was to discover later how fortunate I was to ignore their invitation. They were part of the Children of God, an advance party to England, later to be exposed as a false cult. I was glad I listened to the niggling voice inside me telling me something was wrong.

Time was drawing near for the Amsterdam trip. Tony had come back to the Lord but felt it wasn't right to make the journey. Instead Peter Ward, one of the staff from Northwick Park, was to be my companion. I met him in London and we drove down to the ferry for the journey to Amsterdam and the conference. My nerves were beginning to tell me it was to be a few days I would not forget. And the same nerves jangled at the thought of letting God down in front of so many evangelists from so many different parts of the world. I had a list of blemishes on my Christian calendar already. God had forgiven me – but I didn't want to add to them.

It was the first time I had left England and I hung across the rail of the ferry watching the Belgian shoreline gradually get bigger. As the boat nudged its way alongside the harbour at Ostend we made our way into its bowels to our car, waiting until the front of the boat dropped like a gaping lower jaw and flattened itself into an iron bridge over which we drove on the Belgian soil.

The thrill evaporated a little as we drove on and I realised that Belgium was very little different from England. It wasn't until we began to pass through some of the Dutch villages and spotted the occasional windmill, or clog-clad farm-workers that I felt I was abroad. We arrived in Amsterdam in the evening and after negotiating the narrow, car-packed roads alongside circling canals reached the skyscraper building which was our hotel, the first hotel I had ever stayed in.

Luxury oozed from every brick. We were taken to our room and I stared from the window over the network of gabled buildings and canals shimmering in the night-lights of the Dutch capital.

I wasn't to speak for a couple of days and couldn't stay in the hotel room, especially in the evenings. Night was when I came to life so I wandered off alone to see whether Amsterdam had anything to offer. In the hotel foyer I met some other Christians and we strolled along until we arrived at the Dam, the centre of the city for tourists and commerce. One side of the huge square was a simple monument, a tribute to Dutch victims in the Second World War. People were sitting or wandering round the square and we began to mingle with them, talking about Jesus when we found anyone who spoke English which was often.

I noticed a group of Children of God youngsters singing choruses with a crowd round them. Fascinated I kept watching. I noticed one of the team whom I knew was already supposed to be a Christian appear from the crowd and pretend to ask Jesus into her life, throwing up her hands and shouting 'Hallelujah.' A chorus of 'Hallelujah's' started. All the time they sang and strummed guitars. Before long they moved off, no doubt to pull off their confidence trick in front of other unfortunate bystanders.

I realised just how devilish that sort of behaviour was and how I needed to keep my eyes on Jesus. It was one of the many pieces of the new-life jigsaw puzzle that were slotting into place at this time, encouraging me to weigh-up everything and measure it by the Bible without simply accepting things at face value.

I was beginning to learn that what a person was mattered more than what a person said or did.

Next day some of the Christians I met took me out in their van, an impressive vehicle. It included a mini-fold-down stage and was stacked with Christian literature as well as a loud-speaker system. We drove to Rembrandtpark, named after the seventeenth century painter, parked near the grass and began to sing and testify. Two or three members of the group interpreted as we spoke because many of the folk lying their sleeping bags on the grass were from other countries. The sleepy crowd was preparing for another hectic night. There were hundreds there: a sort of Piccadilly Circus of Europe. As I walked among the young people I spotted many who were on drugs. I chatted to those who could speak English, telling them how God had changed my life.

Later that evening after eating in the hotel I went off on my own to explore. I reached Dam square again and turned right, past the national monument. To the left the huge wooden spire of the Old Church was visible over the roof-tops against the darkening sky, a visible reminder that God cared for the folk of Amsterdam. It was a timely reminder for as I continued on towards the New Market I discovered I was in the red light district: Amsterdam's answer to Soho but far more obvious.

Prostitutes sat in windows rather like tailor's dummies, knitting or painting their nails waiting for callers. As they saw me walk by they paused in their knitting to smile a welcome.

Every so often I passed cafes, their seats and tables spread across the pavements alongside the canals and vying for custom with the girls and the bookstallers who packed their display panels with pornographic magazines of every description. In many ways I was at home, not because of the obvious sin all round me, but because I was able to witness and talk about Jesus and know that the people I was talking to needed to hear the message of his love.

The following evening I was due to give my testimony. During the day I spent time scribbling notes on a piece of paper but despite that aid, when the time came I was nervous. It was an ordeal to face so many mature Christians. As I approached the stage with two thousand faces peering in my direction I discovered that the small table which held the microphone also contained a bright lamp, shining directly into my eyes. I couldn't read a word of my notes. So I spoke . . . I talked of what I had been . . . of how low I had sunk . . . of the feeling of desperation as I realised just how much control crime and drugs had over me. And then I told of the way Jesus lifted me up, a little at a time, out of that pit and began to establish my feet on a firm foundation.

The words seemed to flow. I knew God was with me. I recalled how I had been baptised in the Holy Spirit and how the extra experience had given me a firmer grasp of the things of God and helped me to shake off the remnants of my old ways. It was a thrilling evening.

Frank took me for lunch the following day at the new Japanese hotel in which he was staying and praised God for the night before. He rejoiced that I had described my filling by the Holy Spirit sensitively using the words 'a second blessing'. I realised it often posed problems, although I never did understand why it should. I appreciated Frank talking to me about my testimony. I didn't want patting on the back but it is necessary to give young Christians support and I wanted to do my best for God.

Then it was back to England. The Amsterdam affair was over but I had learned a lot. I had caught a vision for reaching people with the real Lord. I was discovering that many people have a distorted idea of who Jesus is, but they were waiting and eager to hear about the real Jesus, the one who loved and changes lives.

It was a vision I wasn't to lose. It would be honed and refined over the years. It would bear fruit on the streets of London, in prisons, borstals, churches and halls. God had helped me see the lost and given me a burden to reach them with the truth.

A weekend at Northwick Park, visiting old friends and meeting newcomers to the centre, left me unsettled. I talked it over with Frank, explaining that I was beginning to feel I could be doing more than I was in the Billy Graham office and the small groups I was involved with in the London area.

'What would you say if I considered being a staff member at Northwick?' I asked.

Frank turned the possibility over in his mind. To my amazement he didn't laugh. Instead he quietly replied. 'We could give it a try.' We agreed that I would return to Northwick Park later in the year when we had both had more time to consider it.

In the meantime I had been invited to the Filey Christian Holiday Crusade. Run by the Movement for Worldwide Evangelisation, thousands of Christians converged on the camp for that week for Bible teaching, seminar sessions, music and a wide range of Christian activities. Life for the World were having a stand in an exhibition and I was asked to help and also give my testimony at one of the evening meetings. It sounded exciting. As soon as I arrived, I felt the atmosphere to be incredible. Being with so many Christians was something special; I began to realise just what a huge family it was. All kinds of people, all very different, but one in the Lord. Evangelist David Watson was giving the morning teaching sessions, talking about spiritual warfare, and I discovered so many new things from the Bible; I was brimming over. I began to meet people who I had only known previously through letters.

As I woke on the day I was to give my testimony the impact began to tell . . . I fasted throughout the day, and although I usually have stomach pains before an important occasion this time I didn't.

Lindsay Glegg, in his late eighties, was leading the meeting; the singing was strong and emotional; the praying seemed to have extra power. The hall was packed and hundreds of others were in another hall watching on closed circuit television. I knew that to talk about my experience of being baptised in the Holy Spirit would cause conflict – but I felt it had to be done. It was, after all, one of the things God had done for me and a very real experience. I told people how God had changed me and mentioned my experiences in Amsterdam. When it was all over I hoped that I hadn't said anything that would offend too many. I felt peaceful. As I stepped down the stairs off the stage a Baptist minister grabbed my hand and shook it. 'Thanks for sharing what you did,' he beamed. He didn't realise how much he encouraged me. One of the other reasons I was grateful to him was that in going on to the platform, and leaving it, none of the convention leaders had greeted me. It was a disquieting experience.

Idly, I picked a book off a shelf in the bookshop the next day and felt a hand on my arm. A young woman introduced herself. 'I'm Eileen. You won't know me, but we want to ask you something.' She motioned to two other women with her. All three were from a Methodist Church in North London.

'I hope you don't mind but we have never heard of the Holy Spirit in the way you talked about him last night,' she went on. It reminded me of the Christians in Acts who had said the same thing to Paul. The peace I had felt the previous evening again came over me. 'Thank you Lord for the confirmation that I didn't abuse the opportunity you gave me,' I said inwardly. The woman went on, 'I stayed up last night with a few friends until four o'clock in the morning waiting for the Holy Spirit to fall on us in the manner you described. We crept to bed disillusioned. Nothing happened.'

I agreed to meet them in their chalet that evening after the meeting and took with me Tony Copeland and another colleague from Northwick. Tony read a few verses of the Bible and we talked about the baptism in the Holy Spirit and then the three of us laid hands on the women and prayed. It was the first time I had ever laid hands on anyone and I didn't know what to expect. But God met them and before we left most of them were rejoicing in God in a new way.

It was my introduction to the truth that was going to be very real to me: just because people might be offended or annoyed was no reason for not speaking of what God had put in my heart. He blessed that testimony and I have found on other occasions since that any fears I have had about certain subjects have usually been overcome when I have plucked up courage and spoken out.

Not long after this I returned to Northwick Park as a probationary staff member, to learn more tough lessons. Things had changed there and it began to dawn on me that it was not the place for me to be.

I began to identify the real problem: having been an addict I felt it was essential to work with former addicts and help in a rehabilitating sense. But it was becoming painfully obvious it wasn't my ministry. The routine and running of Northwick which had been a blessing when I had been there as a resident suddenly became a cage when I was on the staff. I felt like a youngster trying to squeeze himself back into a cradle. I knew I had made a mistake. One afternoon I packed my bags and left, arriving in London in a real state, not knowing what to do. In the end I found myself wandering across Clapham Common. Feeling foolish I telephoned a former friend, John Harris, and asked if he could put me up for the night. I was invited over immediately and managed to get my old job back in the Billy Graham office. Another lesson had been learnt the hard way: don't move unless you hear God telling you to very clearly.

In my enthusiasm I had jumped the gun.

12: Back to prison

Thanks for your letter and the booklet. To tell you the truth I am not interested in the booklet – I am only interested in you, sir, for your words touched me. Though I feel kind of stupid saying things like that, but I no longer care. I am not a proper Christian. Now I pray for hope.

E. Pucklechurch Remand Centre.

John and his wife Dawn lived at Forest Gate and I was made to feel part of their home. I went to church with them, usually to Kensington Temple, the Elim Church, and immersed myself in my work and in helping where I could.

I kept in touch with Anita and Viv and managed to get a solicitor to help Anita, although it was very evident that the case in which she had become involved with a gang who were pushing Chinese Heroin, would finish with her in prison.

I regularly visited Norman and my old friends at the crypt at St Martins and also joined a girl named Pam visiting addicts in various places. I spent some evenings in Piccadilly Circus where a woman called Joan Askew had been taking soup and sandwiches to the down-and-outs for years. I recalled when I had been an addict on one occasion I had come to in Piccadilly with a pair of shoes near my eyes. I was lying in the gutter. A voice was saying, 'Are you hungry?' It was Joan who gave me a sandwich and a cup of tea. I thought now of those words, 'I was hungry and you fed me; I was thirsty and you gave me water . . . ' (Matthew 25:35 Living Bible).

With Joan I also visited patients in Tooting Hospital, but somehow always felt uneasy . . . it was almost as if I was too close to them to help. I could never seem to get through to them. In the end I decided to give it a miss for a while. But what could I do? I applied to go to Bible College, it seemed the norm for ex-prisoners and addicts (Tony Copeland was now a student) but decided against it when they wanted an agreement that I wouldn't speak in tongues! I couldn't give that assurance, but it confused me again as to my future.

Then John Harris stepped in. He had visited a few prisons to talk or show the film Born to Live (just released at that time). One day he asked me to go with him. I had only been a Christian for about eighteen months and I was used to telling my story by this time but the thought of repeating it inside prison was very different. I prayed about it until finally feeling it was right to go ahead. As I walked behind John through the gate of Wandsworth Prison it seemed unreal. I passed the landing on which my cell had been and the smell hit me: a reminder of the day two years before when I had been a very different person. We clanked up the spiral staircase to the chapel and I thought of the changes those two years had brought. It was truly miraculous. From a drug addict, keen to find his way to Piccadilly Circus and another fix, here I was sane, in my right mind, drug-free and loving Jesus.

I was introduced to the chaplain, Percy Ashford, and we prayed in a small room adjoining the chapel. Then we entered the chapel; it was packed. I guess it held about a hundred men and I sat, transfixed, looking at them. John adjusted the projector and the film started . . . I sat half watching and half worrying about what would follow. What should I say? How many of the men were only here because it was better than being cramped in their cells? What would they think of an old prison mate who'd turned religious? The film flickered off the end of the reel and John clicked off the projector. He spent a few seconds talking about the Life for the World and then introduced me. I walked in front, faced the prisoners, and took a deep breath. I wanted so much to be sensitive to their needs and relate Jesus in a way they would understand.

God took over, as usual! My story poured out, the heartache, the years in prison, the frustration and anguish, the years of captivity to drugs, and the beam of light Christ had brought into my life.

'God managed to change my life, and he can change yours,' I promised. 'You might be stuck in a rut, desperate for a way round the fence which blocks you from God but he can come to you right now.' At points I was close to tears, it was an emotional moment for me to stand in the chapel where I had mocked God by my lack of interest, and acknowledge what he had done for me. At the end I stood on the opposite side of the door to John and shook hands as the prisoners filed out. We had just sung one of Charles Wesley's hymns with the powerful line, 'My chains fell off,' and that was how I felt.

I spotted a familiar face in the procession, a former mate from Borstal. He shook my hand. 'I'm doing ten years. I'm glad you're free.'

'But you can be free, too,' I assured him.

He shrugged his shoulders and shuffled off to his cell. My elation was suddenly soured. How could I help men like him see the love of God and find freedom for themselves?

Leaning on the pub table I traced a line on the murky top with beer spilled from Johnny Probits' glass. Johnny was a London spiv-type, never doing atrocious crimes but almost permanently inside for petty things. I had met him, an old friend, and was trying to explain how he could cross from his old life into the new life Christ was offering. He stared at the diagram I was illustrating my talk with, scraped the bottom of his tankard through it and drained his beer. 'Nar – it wouldn't work wif me,' he grinned. It was the story of my life at this time. Reaching out, and touching nothing and nobody.

I took Johnny to a crusade meeting in the area but he pricked up his ears at the books and records which were offered for sale, ignored the sermon, and then told me it was all a big con. 'Just salesman's talk. They're in it for the money.'

The trouble was I understood what he meant and there was the germ of truth there. I had the same feeling when I took a girl to Wembley Stadium to hear Arthur Blessitt speak. When he asked everyone who was a Christian to raise a hand there didn't seem anyone without a hand raised.

It was another thumping blow to my faith. What was the point? Having been involved in giving my testimony at many crusades and meetings it was suddenly coming home to me just how commercial Christianity could appear to the outsider. I couldn't square it with the way God honoured the crusades. As my mind kept churning round these critical elements it began to dawn on me how cynical I was becoming. I was self-centred and beginning to close my mind to everything.

The Holy Spirit began to work on my mind in a fresh way teaching me to leave the Lord to look after his own business and get on with what God was telling me to do. While my mind was still trying to take that in, the message was reinforced at work.

In the office we were frantically preparing for SPREE '73, a crusade to reach young people in London. Billy Graham came into the office one day and called the staff together. It was a time of tension and heavy workloads.

'If you are not convinced that this is right then move over and let the people who think it is right come in and do the work,' he said; direct and to the point. My respect for the evangelist grew from that day. He was one of the first preachers I had met personally, and he was unafraid to say unpopular things. It put a lot of my problems into perspective.

One of my difficulties was clothing: I couldn't understand why Christians were swayed by fashion in the same way that folk in the world were. And music: it had been an essential background to my life when I was on drugs and was one of the influences which had drawn me back on occasions. Now I was a Christian and cutting myself off from that I suddenly discovered Christian pop stars and Christian records, some of which seemed little different from the music I felt I had been freed from. Christians who gossiped were another area of concern which I had difficulty coping with, though in condemning them I was guilty of the same thing. All these were problems I stumbled over and struggled with . . . but discovered few answers in my Christian youth.

When I heard of a rally in Trafalgar Square, organised by Christians who were concerned at the state of the nation, I decided to join them. I arrived to discover thousands packing the square and the surrounding area for what was later called the Festival of Light. It was amazing, so many Christians and suddenly everyone was of one accord. This was the unity for which I prayed.

I followed the crowd to the follow-up rally in Hyde Park and managed to squeeze my way to the front to join in the singing and listen to Arthur Blessitt, Cliff Richard and others.

That night as I went home the Underground hummed with hymns and choruses. But as the train progressed and Christians got off the singing faded. I often think back to the early part of that journey and the singing: a vision of heaven.

In the office the work kept going on towards SPREE '73 and outside office hours I continued to help where I could. I hadn't lost touch with Eileen, the girl I had prayed with at Filey, and one day she telephoned to ask whether I would talk to some of her friends. With John's support I agreed. They had specifically requested a Bible study on the baptism in the Holy Spirit and armed with my Thompson Chain Reference Bible and a ready list of references I went. Most of the group were Sunday School teachers, one was a policeman, and others had the look of professional people. My nerves were on edge by the time I started to speak to the group gathered in Eileen's flat. But as I ploughed through what seemed a maze of scriptures they listened with growing enthusiasm. No one wanted to ask questions at the end, instead they wanted to be prayed for. There was silence as Val (she had been a missionary and had chipped in with helpful illustrations during the study) and I prayed. Suddenly the heavens seemed to open; wave after wave of praise rose from the group; some spoke in new tongues and everyone seemed to capture a spirit of liberty. We praised God until the early hours of the morning and in the following few weeks as I kept in touch I was encouraged by what the group were doing and experiencing. What I didn't know was that it was preparing me for the next stage of my life. I should have guessed when, from that meeting, another policeman became a Christian and I found myself one day praying with a policeman, magistrates and other ex-prisoners.

But despite encouragements something was still missing and I couldn't place what it was; my life lacked real purpose. I didn't really feel fulfilled. I decided to spend a few days in Sidmouth. Time to relax, look up old friends, and perhaps sort out my feelings. It was a visit that was going to have great repercussions in my life. I hadn't been to Sidmouth for about eight years, but early one morning, I put a few things into a bag, clipped them on to the back of my motor cycle, and set off.

13: The Haven

I've been given a Good News New Testament as I never had a Bible of my own. I hope I will look after it as it is my way of hearing what God is saying. How do I get baptised or confirmed? I would like to be baptised and fully clean.

C. Portland Youth Custody Centre.

As soon as I walked along the promenade at Sidmouth I knew it was where I should be. The fresh sea breeze and the red cliffs rising sheer at either end of the sea front with the town nestling like a gem in the centre. It was an unspoilt town; untouched by the brash commercialism that had tainted so many others.

I arrived around mid-day after my early morning start, and went straight to the beach to soak up the sun and relax.

I wanted to find Fred and Wendy, needing somewhere to stay and they were, after all, two of the only friends I had from the past who somehow, I sensed, would be part of my future. It took an hour or so to get their new address and then I aimed the motor-cycle towards the little village where they were living, East Budleigh. I swept into the village and pulled up as the road broadened out with a row of council houses. I called to a woman walking down the road. 'Do you know where Fred and Wendy Broom live?' Before she could answer I realised it was Wendy. She hadn't recognised me because of my goggles and helmet. 'It's me, Tony – I mean Michael,' I said correcting myself as soon as I had spoken remembering that she wouldn't know me by my more recent names.

'I thought you were dead,' she gasped.

As we went into the house she explained that she and Fred had tried to trace me through all sorts of channels after hearing I had been in Sidmouth years before. But they had drawn a blank everywhere and decided I must have died through drugs.

I walked into the house. I saw Fred, chunky and tough as ever, and their son Gary, now a young boy, plus Steve, their second son. I sipped the tea which Wendy poured for me and we talked. After a while Fred asked: 'Where do you work?'

Up to that point I hadn't mentioned I was a Christian and although I had witnessed in London I now felt acutely embarrassed to volunteer that information. It was alright with others but Fred was the guy I had boozed with, fought alongside, and picked up girls with. 'I work in an office,' I fenced.

'What sort of office?'

My mind raced. I decided to take the plunge. 'In a Christian office.'

'Oh. I was into religion myself once a bit. I was with the Jehovah's Witnesses for a couple of years.' We both left it at that and switched the subject. It was good to see them again. They made me welcome and offered me a bed for the few nights I was to be around. I was delighted to accept.

Next day I went back to the beach. As I lay in the sun I heard music and pricked up my ears . . . hymns. I jumped up and found a group carrying Bibles and singing. I told them I was a Christian and was taken to a coffee bar in the high street. It was a two storey building with a snooker table downstairs and a larger room upstairs, a dark building with character but needing a coat of paint. The musty atmosphere was because it was used only for a few weeks each year as the outreach centre for a team of students.

As we talked I was introduced to Stephen Hayles, the minister of Emmanuel Free Evangelical Church which owned the building. His daughter had been involved in drugs but had been set free and was now part of a Christian music group so he knew about drugs and was interested in my past.

The sleepy little town I had known in my youth was, he told me, the centre of a lot of drug activity. His dream was for a permanent coffee bar as the centre for work among the addicts. It needed the agreement of the church, and someone to run it!

Our minds were running parallel. 'Would you run it?' he

ventured. 'That is if the church leaders agree its use.' The question, even though I sensed it was coming, threw me. 'I'll pray about it,' was all I could manage.

That evening I thought. My mind whirled. I opened my Bible and was struck by the story of the man Jesus had healed. Jesus' words hit me, 'Go back to your family and tell them what God has done for you.' The man had wanted to follow Jesus – he had been sent home to witness there.

I had been faithful in London, now perhaps I was to live for Jesus in the place where I had been in trouble.

The conviction grew: Christ wanted me back in Sidmouth and the coffee bar was to be my work. I told Stephen if he got the go-ahead I was interested.

When I returned to London I was full of excitement and a growing vision. I knew something tremendous was going to happen. Sidmouth was the area of many of my petty crimes. I was going back to demonstrate the power of God to change lives. When I got the letter saying that the church was behind the venture and I was invited to run the coffee bar I was elated. John and Dawn had a farewell meeting for me and I also went to Palmers Green where the folk I had ministered to laid hands on me and committed me to the Lord. I clipped the last few items on to the back of my motor cycle and had a final look at Forest Gate.

Shortly before I'd heard my application to go to another Bible College had been accepted. But the coffee bar burned brighter than college. Something told me it was in Sidmouth that I was going to find the key to my future. God had a plan for me and the coffee bar was to be the first stage in discovering that plan. I was now two and a half years old as a Christian and ready for anything. I kicked the bike into action, released the clutch, twisted the accelerator. I was on my way.

It was ironic that Sidmouth, the town from which I had been sent to Approved School, Borstal and Prison, should be the place where I was called to start the first real work of my life. I couldn't help but grin when I learned the former job of Stephen Hayles, the minister who invited me to take over the coffee bar: he had been a policeman and then a London City Missioner!

I was given a warm welcome by the members of Emmanuel

church, the church to sponsor and support me in many ways over the next couple of years. I sat in the modern, well-lit church, first built in 1933, now re-built, and recalled the miraculous change in my life during the years since I had left Sidmouth. From a hardened criminal running downhill towards more trouble than I could cope with, a drug addict, and a renegade Roman Catholic who had no time for God. Suddenly within the space of two and a half years I had been catapulted into a leadership position. The church, squatting next to a large council estate, was to be my spiritual base and the coffee bar my work-place. A dear old lady from the church offered to look after me and so with lodgings established, I was free to start work.

I wandered into Sidmouth to check over the coffee bar. It was a fair walk but the sea air and the memories of home did me good.

I passed Exeter Cross, the crossroads that had been a meeting place for many of my old gang over the years, past the fish and chip shop on the right and kept walking until the police station came up on my left. It felt good to stroll by knowing I wasn't wanted for anything. The cinema was on the opposite side of the road and a little further down I swung left into a side street where, a few yards down, a battered wooden door marked my new challenge. Inside the door hung a curtain, a compromise intended to keep the biting wind out in the winter and the dust from the road in the summer. An old YMCA building, it had a heritage of outreach over the years and felt comfortable. The outer door creaked as I opened it and, pushing aside the curtain, I stepped into a large room with a set of stairs rising on the far side. To the right was a small kitchen, separated from the room by a bar. Further to the right was a small passage which led to a back room and the single toilet. Upstairs was a large room with low windows looking out over the town. To get across the room I had to negotiate a massive snooker table. I rolled a snooker ball across the table and wondered what I was going to do. The ball ricocheted round the dull green baize until it clipped a cluster of balls at one end, cannoning one of them into the pocket. And that set me thinking. I'd get nowhere without meeting people, so why not start seeing who I could bump into?

At first I met a bit of opposition from people who remembered me from my past. I had stolen money from one man and he had had a difficult time because he had never got his cash back. Even though I had been to court and in some ways paid for my crime I felt that restitution ought to be made. When I offered him a weekly donation out of my meagre £7 a week he was staggered. It took seven or eight months to repay him but my testimony was strengthened as I did so. Others in the town shied away from me at first. 'Clear off, Ralls,' said one man as I walked into the pub to spot old friends, and enemies. After a drink he began to see that I was different. Others thought I had cracked up; some considered it a new form of villainy and waited for the crunch to come; some listened and believed me.

I re-established contact with Fred and Wendy and discovered that they were having a really difficult time. Fred was always a tough character and now I found he had been going off with a younger woman and beating Wendy; that, and a drink problem was hurtling their marriage towards divorce at high speed. 'I do pray,' Wendy told me. 'I pray he'll go out and break his neck.' It was a pattern I was to discover in many of my old friends.

With the support of young people from the church I started to clean up the coffee bar and prepare it for our work. We decided to call it The Haven, so an amateurish notice was painted and stuck on the door.

The snooker table was the first thing to go – it was enormous and took up far too much room. I set myself a rigid timetable in an effort to get the work done quickly; I got up, had breakfast, and spent the rest of the morning in prayer, reading my Bible and talking to God about the future of the work and discussing plans with Him, and praying in tongues. In the afternoons I helped with the clearing-up, painting and decorating, and in the evenings visited friends or new contacts in an effort to reach people for God. I was super-keen, perhaps too much so, and looking back might have upset a lot of people by my bluntness and legalistic way of looking at things.

I discovered a wide range of folk, many on drugs, who had been contacted at some time or other by workers from the coffee bar. As The Haven opened for business the youngsters started to come in, slowly at first, just a trickle, and in greater numbers as the news began to spread.

Christian Unions presented another area for my witness, one

particularly keen one being at Kings' Grammar School.

As the work began to settle down into its own routine different visitors became regular. Doreen worked in the hotels in Sidmouth. A Scots girl, she was mixed up with LSD and various other drugs and was hanging around with a guy who seemed to influence a lot of young girls.

Through Doreen I was introduced to the problems of demonic possession. Late one evening I had been talking to her about Christianity and helping her down from an LSD trip when she demanded she should run to this fellow. I physically held her back, praying and calling on Jesus to release her. In her drugged state she imagined she could hear the man calling her. I realised it was some sort of possession and prayed hard. Finally she pulled through and later became a Christian.

It was tough work. Doreen, for instance, would leave a time of prayer, go to pub and I would have to fish her out. I knew that somehow I had to keep up the pressure and my persistence was rewarded in Doreen's case: she left the area to live with Christian friends of mine and eventually married a Christian guy. Now they are happily bringing up two children.

Battles like that seemed to be constantly pressing me and yet there was not a lot of fruit to be seen. I got quite despondent. Then, one day, Steve arrived. A Kings School pupil, Steve had been reading some books by Erich von Daniken about God being an astronaut and arrived to argue and debate with me. We talked for hours and just as I was questioning whether I was wasting my time Steve returned to tell me, 'You're right, you know. Will you pray with me?' Amazed I prayed and wondered. He jumped on his bike and wobbled up the road shouting 'Praise the Lord,' and 'Hallelujah'. I wasn't sure whether I believed his conversion or not.

But Steven began to bring in friends from school and within weeks three had been converted leading to our first prayer meeting in the coffee bar. I didn't know the significance of Steve's new life for some time but should have guessed something at the prayer meeting. Stephen Hayles read from the Bible and spoke from Ephesians six about spiritual warfare. There were six of us at the meeting but suddenly it seemed The Haven was on the map. Days later, Eileen, my friend from Filey and

London, arrived at the coffee bar to say she had got a job in Sidmouth and wanted to help us in her spare time.

More and more people started to come. It was wall-to-wall with teens at times. The midweek prayer meeting soared from that initial six to fifty or sixty and even a hundred on occasions, mainly youngsters who had been converted as a result of the work of the coffee bar and many with no church connections. There were also a few older people.

It was electrifying, although there were problems. It wasn't easy for church-based youngsters to handle the atmosphere and pressure of working with such rank outsiders but some managed and became effective witnesses in the streets of Sidmouth. Others stopped coming to concentrate on the church youth groups.

Thursday nights were our focal point with speakers such as Eric Delve, Len Moules and Arthur Wallis chatting to as many youngsters as we could pack in. Some of us would fast all day and I'm confident that that practical witness to God helped. The meetings often went on for up to three hours with plenty of time for open worship and prayer.

And teenagers were finding Jesus Christ. I was excited. I was also being stretched for there were constant questions being hurled at me and I felt a compulsion to discover some sort of answer even if I had to check it out over a few days.

I began a regular teaching course, including baptism, being filled with the Holy Spirt, and sharing the gifts of the Spirit, particularly healing and deliverance. It became regular that people were converted and often baptised in the Spirit and then in water at Emmanuel church.

God was using the young people who were all out for him, unafraid to witness and confident that things would happen. I found myself co-ordinating all their efforts so that God could move at speed. The seafront became our other pulpit, an open air point of contact with many. And at holiday times when Sidmouth was packed many of the converts returned to other parts of the country to live out the new life they had discovered on holiday.

But all the time one personal area of desperation was nagging me, Fred and Wendy. As I visited them regularly it was obvious they were further apart. Fred's previous involvement with Jehovah's Witnesses had disillusioned him about anything to do with God. But he would talk and I was anxious not to lose the thread of our friendship so we went to a pub together every week. I didn't like alcohol but it was the only way to keep in touch. One night our conversation began to stretch beyond the normal; Fred questioned me with more than his usual vigour and candour. He probed and prodded until four o'clock in the morning and suddenly asked me to pray for him. I was staggered: hard-nut Fred wanting to be a Christian. Tears welled in my eyes as we bowed and prayed and as Fred started to pray his own confession and ask Christ to forgive him I knew that it was real. I felt so humble to be part of his conversion.

Immediately he had finished Fred looked at me with a look of joy, raced up the stairs, and called to Wendy, 'I've become a Christian.' Wendy was asleep. She roused, mumbled, 'Good. I want to sleep,' and rolled over, pulling the bed-clothes over her ears. It was a night I will not forget. As I made my way the few miles from Fred's village to my own lodgings I was singing all the way. That was what being a Christian was all about: the thrill of seeing someone change completely. It had happened to me; now it had happened to Fred. Suddenly all the effort at the coffee bar was worth it. If the whole reason for moving to Sidmouth had been for that one night I would have been grateful. Just one thing remained to be done: we needed to win Wendy. But surely after big, burly Fred that wouldn't be difficult?

It became obvious after some weeks that the Christian edge Fred and I always managed to bring into our conversation was driving Wendy further into a corner.

I began to realise just how she felt; years of violence, drink and infidelity had made her suspicious of her husband. She was worried that it was another fad. We decided not to talk about Jesus in front of Wendy again and agreed that she would have to see Jesus through the changed life-style of her once tough husband. It was a strategy that worked. Wendy grew more and more curious and one night when she accompanied us to a baptismal service at Emmanuel she came to the point. 'I want to become a Christian,' she confessed. It was another dramatic moment. The two were baptised together and later insisted on making their marriage vows again in the church. 'We might have been legally married but it wasn't real until we became Christians,' Fred explained.

Fred's elderly ex-miner father became a Christian and was baptised because of their witness, just a year before he died. That in itself was significant since he had been violent himself and once tore up his wife's Bible when he caught her reading it and praying.

Fred found the going tough for some time. He still had violent spells and depressions but as God changed him more those spells wore off and today he's a solid Christian, a local councillor, and a popular builder whom people can trust. His children are loved and secure and the marriage is welded firm with an incredible love to withstand the many storms of life. In fact that night of prayer in Fred's home enabled God to pluck out a friend who is often a shoulder for my own spiritual burdens. Of course life wasn't all success: another friend, Bill, the third person in the Fred and Tony trio, made a commitment on one occasion but didn't stay the course.

Life at The Haven was hectic. One evening three girls, all daughters of the local vicar, came in and were baptised in the Spirit. God is very much a God of the individual; Helen and Linda jumped all over the place and Rachel received very quietly. It was one of many incidents, but one which was to have a profound effect on my own life later. I was to marry one of the three. A bank manager arrived one evening with his wife and asked us to pray for the Holy Spirit to fill them. The religious education teacher at a local school was converted and baptised in the Spirit and later went on to become a missionary. Then there was Dave. He was considered the village idiot but he became a Christian, found his life changed, and is now married and living happily with his family in West Germany. And so it went on. There were tough decisions that had to be taken as well. Often I had to bar youngsters from the coffee bar because of their disruptive influence and the first time it had to be done I was physically sick, realising the need for discipline yet fearful for their spiritual futures.

I was also made to broaden my personal spiritual horizons.

In London I had mixed with evangelicals but now I found the Mother Superior from the local convent was occasionally in our meetings. She often invited me to the convent to speak and pray with the children there. God was showing me something about meeting people who knew Him through Jesus, without being worried about doctrinal differences. The Body of Christ was more important than theological problems. They could look after themselves.

The coffee bar was usually open from noon until midnight and I would be there well after closing time, talking or praying with some of the visitors. It was those extended hours that began to wear me down physically as my time at The Haven reached the end of the second year. Apart from the constant tiredness I was puzzled about the membership I had at the local church and was further frustrated because I had started smoking again.

Some months before I had moved to a fifteen-roomed guest house, Sussex House, in the centre of Sidmouth. One of the boys who had become a Christian at the coffee bar was the son of the owners and his mother, Ruth, recommitted herself to the Lord through his conversion. Normally she closed the guest house in the winter, but when she realised we were coming more and more into contact with people with accommodation problems, she let some of them live there during those winter months. My move to the guest house, however, put me under another strain; when I finished work in the coffee bar I returned to face the spiritual problems of the people living there. Life was a constant spiritual battleground, plenty of giving, little receiving.

There was an additional dilemma: I had become engaged. When I had prayed for the Holy Spirit to fill the three daughters of the local vicar I had no idea I would fall in love with Linda but I did. And Linda, an academically brilliant girl who had been awarded a place at Cambridge University, loved me. We were engaged for three months before telling anyone, mainly so as not to disrupt the work among the young people. We also fixed our wedding day a year ahead, knowing that it would mean Linda would have to turn down her university place. This proved difficult. I was about thirty at the time; had been fond of pointing out to people that Paul the apostle said it was good to be single; and Linda was giving up the chance of a lifetime to go to Cambridge. But we were confident we were doing what God wanted.

I spent hours praying it through. After all, I had a hardened criminal record and Linda was a fine Christian girl, daughter of the vicar. She seemed too good for me.

I recalled a friend coming to see me when I lived in London shortly before moving to Devon. 'Don't worry about who you'll marry,' he said to me. 'God will provide the right person.' It was a prophetic word that came back to me as I puzzled over my relationship with Linda.

We prayed and sang in the Spirit together and worked in the coffee bar. In the past all the women I had known had been objects of sexual desire. Suddenly I loved a woman and she was to become my wife.

Obviously I found her sexually attractive but somehow this was back-to-front. We were drawn together in the Spirit. I had used girls in the past and was grateful to God for giving me this lovely girl to be my wife, and forgiving me my past. It was another indication that my life was to change again. It was to be re-directed in more than that one way. For I began to realise gradually that my work was finished in the coffee bar. And when a door had closed in the past another had always opened. The new door wasn't long in revealing itself.

14: Sussex House

My cell mate sends his regards. Do you remember him from Sussex House eight years ago? He is now doing a four for robbery and burglary but when he gets out will drop you a line.

K. Camphill Prison, near Newport, Isle of Wight

The decision about leaving The Haven was taken out of my hands. Pressure of work, plus some other problems between myself and the church, meant that I was beginning to be unhappy and felt I should withdraw my membership. It was not an easy decision to make and I made it only after consulting a number of friends. But it meant that I was relieved of the leadership of the coffee bar anyway, leaving me very bitter. Now I regret the bitterness, although God seemed to use the division it caused in the church to his advantage. Losing the coffee bar set in motion the wheels which opened the other door: Sussex House.

A large three-storey building a few yards from the promenade in Sidmouth, Sussex House was ideally placed. At the western end of the town it overlooked a car park, tennis courts, the picturesque rust-coloured cliffs poised over the sea on one side and the rolling green Devon hills in the other direction. On the first floor a miniature balcony stuck out precariously from the side of the building over a double bay window and above the balcony an ornamental weather shield kept the worst of the rain clear of the windows. I found the switch from running the coffee bar to looking after people in a living-in situation vastly different, although Ruth continued to look after much of the practical side.

Because many in the house were there because of drugs or prison problems I soon found myself dredging up all the knowledge I had acquired in my own past in an effort to help. Life was complex, full, exciting and tiring.

I didn't help myself, of course, retaining a bitter attitude towards the events of the previous few months: my sad departure from Emmanuel church and the losing of the coffee bar. I began to read the Bible avidly to see whether it had anything to say to me. Of course it did.

As I read the Old Testament prophets I realised that they had often been despised even when they were doing what they felt was right in God's eyes. Jesus himself was rejected for doing his work in his way. I felt confident in what God wanted me to do and began to pass through a time of bitterness and darkness. It was a wilderness experience which strengthened me for some of the difficulties that lay ahead in my life.

If I had doubts about the structure of church denominations I had no doubt about the need for the Body of Christ and for Christians to exercise the gifts the Holy Spirit had endowed them with. Gradually people started to flow into the house: the fifteen bedrooms were usually full and the pressure intense. I had to learn two things: to live by faith (there was no income other than what some of the tenants paid and gifts from Christians); and to minister to a wide range of needs while at the same time being prepared for the ill-feeling that itself could generate. Some accused me of being a homosexual because we had many single boys in the home; others claimed I was sleeping with the girls because there were girls; and some folk even went so far as to claim we were stashing away thousands of pounds from the folk living there.

If I hadn't been at such a low spiritual ebb I would have laughed a lot more often.

Fred and Wendy came to help for a time but Fred was a practical person who eventually realised that his calling in life was building and being a witness in that, not in residential work. So he returned to his work, still giving us a hand whenever something needed fixing. He did, in fact, start his own building company from his home in East Budleigh. As the years past he and Wendy were to be spiritual rocks to me.

Ruth was a bundle of energy and other voluntary helpers appeared from time to time to help out. It was the first time I had lived in close proximity to anyone since my Northwick Park days; I was the leader of the work and the buck stopped with me. I still had many rough edges that needed knocking off. And while I was being smoothed over people were being helped. I'm always amazed how God can use us whatever our circumstances and however spiritually inadequate we feel.

Bob Butcher had spent fifteen years in prison, including Strangeways, and had a drugs and alcohol problem. He lived with us for a few months while we prayed and taught him about the new life God offered. Eventually he moved out to work in local hotels and then left the area altogether.

It could have ended there, but didn't. Years later a man and woman came up to me and started to talk: it was Bob, and his wife; happily married for six years and Bob a Methodist lay preacher in Seaton. I praised God then for all that he had been doing those years ago in Sussex House. Bob remembered one thing from the past. He had bought a very expensive card for his fiance as she was at that time and had been roundly condemned by many around him for wasting money. I had told him 'What you have done is precious.' I didn't realise that ten years later Bob, a stable Christian, would be reminding me of that occasion.

Carol was one of the girls we helped. She came to Sussex House and appeared to be just skin and bone wrapped in a huge cloak. She had been involved in drugs and had côme to attempt to put her life together. Gradually, over a period of time, she made a commitment to the Lord and began to grow as a Christian. It was like watching a flower open in slow motion; she became a radiant Christian and eventually married Tony, one of the guys who had also come to the house to get off drugs.

Others were not quite so easy and some drew me into areas of Christian ministry I hadn't entered before. One girl often went into fits of screaming for no apparent reason. As I watched and observed I began to piece together the incidents that sparked the outbursts; it was certain flying insects or a tense situation. Something began to tell me that the secret was locked in her mind, an incident from her past. I prayed with her for deliverance from the past and she was completely cured. It introduced me to what is now a commonplace counselling technique but was then something not often heard of, certainly in Christian circles.

A lovely girl was to be married but still felt the evil influence of a man she had associated with many years before. I took Matthew 18:18 at face value: 'What you loose on earth will be loosed in heaven.' and as we prayed she also found freedom from the past.

Another girl, also named Carol, taught us another lesson. She was a young Christian who seemed to radiate God's love; always praising God and singing and speaking in tongues. She seemed to have a dynamic faith . . . until we discovered she had been regularly stealing money from many of the people at the home! Amazingly she came to me one day and asked for an explanation of some Scriptures she had read. She felt she had to choose either the sun or the darkness. I explained her choice was between God and the devil, light and darkness.

Sadly she rejected the warning and I had to ask her to leave after talking to her firmly about her behaviour. I felt I could do no more; and the well-being of the house seemed more important than trying to control one girl who rejected our help.

By now the wedding day was approaching for Linda and I. Then the bombshell fell: Ruth announced that she would be leaving Sussex House to start a home on her own doing similar work. Sussex House was to continue in a similar form but it meant that within days of our wedding Linda and I would be in sole command. The thought was frightening. But Linda rose to the challenge. Opting out of her place at Cambridge University had cost her dear: she had been working in a factory soldering bits of wire together and on occasions doubling as a waitress in a hotel in the evening as I was hardly earning anything. Now she agreed to run the house with me after the wedding. And if that wasn't enough she was also a sounding board for the puzzled ideas which were still thumping their way round my own head. Linda was patient and because we tried to put God first in our relationship, he seemed to honour it.

With Ruth's help I managed to pass my driving test and with the old banger I bought was glad to be rid of the crash helmet and paraphernalia of the motor cycle, particularly in bad weather.

The local authorities now and then put people into our care: often I would appear at courts all over the country to speak on someone's behalf, and people were regularly allowed to go free into our care when by all accounts they deserved a long prison sentence. The more I appeared around the courts in my new role as protector and helper (that took a bit of getting used to for some court officials) the more the police and probation officers would call me to help with particularly difficult people.

Finally the wedding day came. It was January 1, 1976 and I had been a Christian for six years. What a start to a New Year. We had agreed to be married at Linda's father's church, the parish church in Newton Poppleford, and it was to be a wonderful occasion. Linda walked down the aisle as the congregation sang 'We are gathering together unto him,' and there was a freedom and fellowship which was thrilling. The girl who prepared the flowers had been through Sussex House and that was one of many seals on the occasion.

After a time of deep depression and pressure I realised I was, despite the problems, surrounded by many Christian friends. God had been so good to me. People were there representing each of the years I had been a Christian. From a drug addict, criminal, always alone I was finding myself in a drastically different world, and being married to a wonderful girl. As we took the vows I saw the love in Linda's eyes and could only praise God.

I went to the wedding with a few pence in my pocket, not really knowing what we would do about a honeymoon. But as people came up congratulating us envelopes were slipped into my pocket. As we drove away from the reception I discovered they contained enough money for the two week honeymoon we had talked about: a country-wide tour introducing Linda to friends from the past.

We climbed into the big old car and trundled round the countryside excited and happy with life and with each other. Unfortunately the fortnight ended too soon and then work started.

Linda found herself the housekeeper of a fifteen bedroom

hotel full of needy people; and I was often away. I don't know how she coped so well. On one occasion I had been visiting Fred and Wendy and telephoned Linda to see how things were going. 'Everything's fine,' she exclaimed lightly. 'The fire brigade have just gone, the police are here and they are taking away the coloured lad who was living with us. He's a suspected typhoid carrier.' I chuckled and put the phone down and resumed my conversation with Fred. When I got home later that evening I discovered Linda hadn't been joking. It had been true. An alcoholic who was with us had set some curtains on fire and two fire engines had roared up to put out the flames. While they were there the police had called to take away the youth. He had clung to Linda's skirt, begging her not to allow them to take him. He was also discovered to be an illegal immigrant. It was beginning to be all part of a day's work.

Meanwhile Ruth had bought her other house and managed to open that to guests, relieving us of some of our visitors which eased the pressure somewhat.

I was constantly staggered at how people found out about us. One man walked up in the throes of an LSD trip. He had seen a cross burning in the sky above the house, he said. We spent the evening talking and in the early hours of the morning he came to know Christ as saviour. He later brought his wife and two children to live with us for a while as they tried to put their lives back together. They had been living in a tent on a hill overlooking Sidmouth. His was one of the more miraculous ways individuals discovered our whereabouts.

Other visitors were troublesome. One girl left us and appeared some months later on the doorstep threatening to cut her wrists and scream to everyone that the Christians had let her down unless we took her back. Another smashed all our windows before the police carried him away. Each day brought a new twist.

Spiritually Linda and I were getting stronger. It wasn't ideal, of course, for any married couple, but we learned to adapt. There were times, however, when the tension came between us and our marriage rocked. But that, unlike the perfect marriages portrayed on television, was life. And we had to learn how to cope.

With my disjointed background it was not easy to fit into married life. I had had a lifetime of pleasing myself and even the majority of the Christian work I had been engaged in contained elements of personal satisfaction. So to be suddenly involved in pleasing someone else, my wife, was difficult.

I had no real family background to lean on for examples. Certainly I demanded too much of Linda in the early days, looking for a spotless home, inviting meals, and satisfaction for my own personal whims. It took time to realise that I was asking for the impossible: in Sussex House it was even more impossible.

It wasn't long before Linda became pregnant, showing the evidence of the new life inside. This was to be an experience for me: the first flesh and blood relation I had had since I was a child. My dear friend Tony Copeland, he'd then changed his name to Tony Cauchi, came to see me with his wife and baby. He demonstrated his enthusiasm for the little life by holding her aloft over his head. I watched her be sick down the back of his neck!

From funny faces and gurgling noises he changed dramatically. I couldn't help but laugh and register that babies are not always happy, smiling infants.

As the birth approached I began to worry. People were still jostling for a place in the house and I was making mistakes. John was one of them. He was on drugs and because of his involvement with a girl in the house I had to ask him to leave after warning him several times not to bring drugs into the house. I was called to a nearby hotel later where he had locked himself into a room and was threatening to commit suicide. He refused to open the door so I shoulder-charged it and smashed my way in. It was almost a fatal mistake – he swung a huge spanner at my head. I managed to twist out of the way as it swished past my ear. It took four of us to restrain him and take him to hospital; throughout the journey he was trying to attack me as I drove the car. When we arrived at the hospital he calmed instantly and spoke plausibly to the staff explaining that there was nothing wrong. Eventually he was to blow his own head off with a shotgun and I felt in many ways I had let him down.

Chris was another lad who looked promising. A drug addict,

he saw something different in us the second he walked into Sussex House. But it didn't stop him going back to his old life and eventually throwing himself to his death off a high balcony after being persuaded by so-called friends to take LSD.

Wendy was an unmarried mum who came to us when her boyfriend started to beat her up badly. He was in prison when she arrived but when his sentence ended he traced her to the mother and baby unit where we had placed her and persuaded her to go off with him. Two years later she was abandoned in a house in which they had been squatting.

Only now was I beginning to see more and more the spiritual warfare in which we were engaged. Just as people began to get their lives straight the devil attacked and laid traps for them.

And it was as bad for Linda and myself. We didn't have a lot of time together, and even though we had been married a year, didn't seem to be getting to know each other as there was always something that needed doing.

Amid all that uncertainty our first child, Abigail was born. Linda's sister Helen had moved in with us to help with the work of running the house since it was getting too much for Linda as the birth approached. Linda was having a hard time and losing weight. She went to hospital for tests a few weeks before the baby was due and we sat back to wait the results, planning to have the baby in the local hospital at Sidmouth with the help of our local doctor. The tests were on Monday. The following day we were sitting down in the early evening, for once a quiet time in the house, when the telephone rang.

When I answered it was for Linda. I was relieved it wasn't one of the obscene calls we got occasionally. 'It's for you,' I called wondering who would be asking for my wife. As she started to listen and talk I realised something was wrong. From the one-sided conversation I guessed it was the hospital and they wanted Linda in immediately. As she placed the telephone back on its cradle I asked, 'What's wrong?' 'It's the baby. If I don't go to Exeter Hospital now I might lose it.' We didn't waste time. While Linda was shoving a few items into a suitcase I got the car out and we made for the Royal Devon and Exeter Heavitree Hospital.

We arrived later that evening. I slumped into a chair next to

Linda's bed to sleep. Bleep, bleep – the piercing noise woke me with a start. The machine strapped to Linda was signalling alarm. A nurse bustled over and switched it back into more subdued action.

Time dragged on with the occasional nurse popping in to chat to Linda and the machine bringing my rest to an end a couple more times before daylight brought the early-morning hospital rituals to life. It wasn't until late the following night that Linda started having contractions. I began to pray in earnest because it was obviously not going to be a normal birth. Because we had changed hospitals I was allowed to stay with Linda; a joy I wouldn't have had at Sidmouth. I stood at the top of the bed watching the nurses busying about, occasionally coming to check on Linda or asking a question.

They had decided that because of the risk of the baby dying through lack of oxygen they wouldn't delay the birth for normal processes so they did what I believe was a vacuum birth: they used a pump to suck the baby clear of the womb, after inducing the birth.

As the medical staff operated efficiently I was asked to leave the room. 'I can handle it,' I reassured them and insisted on staying as I thought Linda needed me. Throughout her ordeal I had my hands on Linda's head, watching every movement and praying in tongues under my breath.

As the wrinkled prune of a baby appeared I felt the excitement of seeing new life. Within seconds, however, the flush of excitement was tempered. The baby was taken away to be placed in an incubator and I noticed she seemed an unusual dark colour and her neck looked twisted.

Bravely, and on reflection, stupidly, I told a nurse, 'I'll love her even though she's deformed.' The nurse gave me a strange look. 'Deformed? There's nothing wrong with your daughter, young man. That's just a muscle weakness in her neck.' My spirits rose again.

Linda, alert all the time, began to chat as they wheeled the little cradle-shaped incubator alongside the bed and plugged it in. We looked at our little daughter. Suddenly I realised the significance of the day.

'Linda, it's your birthday.'

'So it is,' she replied. Then it dawned on us both at the same time. It was Linda's twenty-first birthday and Abigail and her mother would always share birthdays in the future.

With unlimited visiting allowed, the hospital became a meeting place for former drug addicts and prisoners as my old friends and people from Sussex House trailed in to see Linda and Abigail. I don't know what the nurses thought. I stayed in Exeter for a few days with a friend, visiting Linda during the day, and then took her back to Sussex House.

Helen had been coping marvellously in our absence but now it became too much. She was, after all, only seventeen. Within a few weeks she had gone back to her parents and Linda was flung into the breach, but too weak to cook. We prayed desperately hard; we had people to feed.

My prayers were interrupted by a knock on the door. Another man wanting to live with us. More trouble, he was an alcoholic. However, I felt I couldn't turn him away, and as we talked I discovered why – he was a chef. God was at work again!

Just as changing circumstances had been the hint that things were to alter once before I began to sense over the next few months that another change was on its way.

The owners of Sussex House wanted to sell the property and a hint of our own future came when I began to counsel an elderly man who was staying with us, trying to shake off a drink habit.

My dealings with him brought me into contact with Commander Metters, a grand old Christian I had met before. In the course of our discussions he offered Linda and myself a house in a place called Uffculme, in Devon, twenty-five miles from Sidmouth.

I went to see the house, Twenty Acres, on a wet, windy day. It was a mile or so into the country surrounded by an acre of land. Despite the weather we decided to move there. Our prayers to the Lord for guidance in the future had been answered again.

Sussex House was being sold and we were able to take some of the furniture with us. I hired a lorry and with the help of a few friends started to load furniture on to it. It was going to be a long day I reckoned, there were four trips to make along twenty-five miles of winding country lanes, so narrow that the lorry's wing mirrors were brushed off by the encroaching hedges on the first journey.

Eventually, at four o'clock in the morning the delivery was complete. Linda and Abigail had been packed into the cab on one of the earlier runs and as I staggered into Twenty Acres at the end of the final drive I sank into a chair. My weary eyes searched the room, crammed with furniture not yet arranged, packing cases stacked jauntily in one corner, Abigail sleeping peacefully in her little cot. Life was taking another turn. I was responsible for a real family; what direction was God going to lead me in now?

15: Twenty Acres

Since I let God come into my life everything has gone well for me. I have prayed to God every night to help me and my friends. I am a one parent family – I lost my wife through an overdose of tablets. I have just heard some good news, I have got parole. My children and myself are all excited about it. I will continue to go to church on my release.

J. Wakefield Prison.

We had hardly unpacked our boxes and arranged the furniture at Twenty Acres before the first man with a drink problem was knocking at the door for help. The house was much smaller than Sussex House, so six people was the maximum we could take, but it didn't take long to reach that figure. Most had drinking backgrounds.

I began to realise that I was inviting people in without thinking enough about it. Many were passing through the house and leaving unchanged. My mistakes were becoming more obvious to myself also. We had so many men and women staying with us over the course of time with the coffee bar and Sussex House, it seemed we had never been free from responsibility. I was drained spiritually and had become hardened and cynical about people. I knew I needed a break from residential work. One major mistake concerned an older man whose daughter was in care. The man was staying with us and I did not realise just how dependent he was becoming on us until it was almost too late. Just as I'd relied on drugs earlier in my life he relied on Linda and myself. I wanted him to strike out on his own and to trust God more than he trusted us. I thought that if I could find him a home of his own and get his daughter back to him the security would help his rehabilitation. I was wrong.

In my impetuous enthusiasm I merely paved the way for incest. On reflection I realise I had tried to put too much responsibility on him before he was capable of taking it. I was too keen to act and not keen enough to listen to God telling me what to do.

As the alcoholics drifted in and out I started to consider Linda and my future. A job was obviously needed so I began to look around. We also needed time on our own. We weren't in fellowship with a church at this time; one of our few links with Christians was through Commander Metters, now eighty, whose experience as a Christian was an enormous help. Rosie and Mick still kept in touch as well and these friends were a great support. Spiritually I didn't know what to do although my first job gave me a broad hint: I worked on a farm helping to erect farm buildings and it wasn't long before I realised I just wasn't cut out for practical work. I was strong enough but somehow every board I nailed was crooked; I fell into every hole around; and when I parked the tractor at the top of a hill one day I watched in horror as it gracefully reversed itself, and crashed through a fence. That same day I fell into a hole full of icy water and the farmer's wife kindly loaned me a pair of his socks and Wellington boots. The farmer, in his droll manner, pointed out it didn't seem right, me walking round in his socks and boots after smashing his fence!

I was working with two men: one a Christian and the other not. But my experience was being extended because I soon realised that the non-Christian had some remarkable gifts, patience and encouragement, which I would have loved to have had. I was embarrassed at being paid for a job I knew I was incapable of doing so I looked for something else.

My next job was in a meat factory, splitting the carcasses of pigs with a sort of buzz-saw, slicing meat and packaging it. I started at five or six in the morning, often working twelve hours a day under artificial lighting, wearing white overalls, white boots, and a white helmet. I worked with rough and ready blokes who tested my testimony and, since it was a union closed-shop, also gave me an insight into some of the difficulties workers face.

It was a dry time spiritually and emotionally. I was still

trying to work many things out in my mind, not least the problems we had experienced with the church. Church traditions didn't seem right to me and Linda was feeling the strain of my emotional hunt.

To pass time away in the evening I bought a guitar and taught myself a few chords. As I strummed I discovered that words and tunes came to me so I started to write them down; it led to me making a long playing record later in life.

It was the guitar that first gave me the opportunity to begin to work in prisons. I spent my lunch hours at the meat factory practising and began to feel a burden for the lads in borstal and prison whom I had known. As a result I wrote letters to the chaplains at prisons and borstals where I had done time asking whether they would allow me to return to sing and talk about the change in my life. I don't know whether I expected an answer or not. In fact my first invitation was to Exeter Prison from the chaplain, Rev Ivor Halliwell, who has since become a close friend.

I arrived at the prison with my guitar packed into its case and the words for my full repertoire of half-a-dozen songs, all in the three or four chords I could handle. Not being a minister I felt my only way into prison was as a gospel singer. It was nerve-racking as he introduced me to the hundred or so men who had gathered in the chapel to listen. It was my first public performance. My throat was dry and my hands clammy. I twisted my fingers into the shape for the chord of C (the most basic) and twitched my right hand across the strings. I managed a couple of songs and then, horror. The guitar went out of tune. I twiddled the keys but no matter how I tried I couldn't tune the instrument. In panic I beckoned to one of the prisoners whom I had met and who I knew played the guitar. He climbed on to the platform, made an effort to tune it and failed. Whether deliberately or not I shall never know.

I propped the guitar against the wall and sang without accompaniment, my face growing a deeper shade of red with every note. 'What can you do with that, God?' I cried inwardly to myself as I finished.

The men were attentive as I spoke for a short time and then Ivor stood and began to speak. He touched on man's foolishness and God's wisdom . . . mentioned that God can use things and people that don't seem valuable by the world's standards. I listened with joy and watched as it obviously impressed many of the men. Two became Christians that night. God, through Ivor, was sealing my prison ministry.

As I left Exeter Prison, the place where years before I had smashed a cell in my violence, a new vision was born: I simply had to reach men who were as lost and powerless as I had been all those years before. I wanted them to have the freedom and new life I possessed.

I was able to return to Exeter and given permission to speak to some prisoners. At first I was given a lot of liberty to talk to various prisoners about my faith until I bumped into a prison officer who remembered me and obviously questioned the radical change. From then on I was restricted to visiting through the normal system, by getting a visiting order from prisoners themselves, which meant I could only see one man at a time in the visiting room.

Another invitation had come my way: this time to Portland Borstal where Andrew Marsden was chaplain. He would be an enormous influence on my life both in opening up the prison ministry to me and in helping me to minister within the system. My unhappy relationship with church life could dangerously spill over into prison work if I wasn't careful. I had to learn to handle the authority structure in prison and work within it rather than fight it.

I began to go to borstal on a regular basis thanks to Andrew's encouragement; once a month to begin with, building up to once a fortnight and then even more regularly. It was one area of my life which was successful. In other areas I was having trouble. My job at the meat factory had to come to an end because I had developed a handicap in my wrist which prevented me from working properly. It was the constant cutting action that did it. I was, they told me, too old to start that sort of work!

A few weeks on the sick made me appreciate what many unemployed were going through but it was a dark time for my personal life.

Being on our own (we had decided not to have any more

visitors) brought to the surface many problems previously hidden because other people were always around. Linda and I quarrelled a lot and I would be quite violent.

We had our second daughter by then, Naomi, born two hours after Linda had the first birth pangs. I was thrilled at first but after losing my job with all the frustrations that brought I was beginning to endure both children rather than enjoy them.

All the immaturity in my life was beginning to surface again, something I had observed over the years but had never completely come to terms with. The responsibilities of being a father and husband didn't come easy. Linda was wonderful, faithful, and stood by me despite all the torment, though the constant strain was beginning to tell on her. There were times of joy, however, like the time we decided to try self-sufficiency and had goats, turkeys, rabbits and all kinds running round the grounds. We even dug half an acre of land to grow our own vegetables. But it was never as easy as it reads in books.

It was the time in my life when God did the biggest remodelling job of all second to my conversion. Because of my background I knew nothing of fatherhood and reading books gave me ideas but also a feeling of guilt: I felt I was borrowing these ideas. Although I was always keen to help others I was very reticent to ask for help for myself.

The prison ministry began to help me see a new direction and with it came a gradual easing in the problems in all the areas of my life.

After three months out of work I was offered a job in a breakers' yard; tough, all-weather work stripping parts off cars. It suited me, since I could do the hours I wanted and be free to visit prisons and borstal when I wanted. As more and more openings came it was an ideal situation. It was a mucky job, I arrived home plastered in grease and oil. I was out in all weathers lying under cars or using the power of the fork lift tractor to raise a useless vehicle so that I could dismantle parts underneath.

All the while I was visiting men in Exeter Prison regularly with an occasional foray to Dartmoor when men moved there. I was also a regular visitor to Portland Borstal, developing a useful work under the guidance of Andrew.

Linda and I took people into our home occasionally but only for short terms. We had a telephone call from a London church one day asking us to give a roof to a man. But soon after arriving he started to throw things around the room until I controlled him by force. Later I learnt he had been violent towards children and women and I lost confidence in the Christians who asked me to take him in. It would have been honest to have told us his background. As always it seemed we were a dumping ground to relieve local churches of their responsibilities.

An old friend, Anita Hydes, the girl I used to hang around with in the East End, had got in touch. I decided to write to her and a friend had delivered the letter to her in hospital where she was seriously ill with septicaemia. At twenty-nine she had many ulcers and a clot on the groin caused by drugs, and doctors could do little for her. She had been an addict for years and the long-term effects had begun to eat away her body. She agreed to spend a week with us – a sort of holiday; the first time she had been outside London in her life apart from prisons and borstals. When I met her I was shocked. She was a shell of a person, hardly able to walk and obviously near the end of her life.

She stayed with us a fortnight and then went back to London. We had talked a lot but nothing seemed to sink in. I tried to persuade her to give up life in London and stay with us where she might have a chance of saving her life but she refused. The lure of London and drugs was too strong. As I watched her depart I felt a deep dissatisfaction; I knew God wanted to do something special for Anita but what and how? Eighteen years on drugs, fourteen as a registered addict, occasional prostitution, and a lesbian life-style: her life was a wreck. But would she let God in? I took her to Exeter Station and watched her through the window as the train started its journey to London. Would she return? Would she give in to God's calling? Was there anything else I could do?

The call from Anita was brief: she would come and stay with us again for a while. It was her way of showing that she wanted to pull away from the drug scene. I was well pleased; it was an opportunity to help her spiritually. Living with us she would only take the drugs prescribed for her and would be away from the influence of her London friends. She also had a couple of court cases pending, one a conspiracy charge relating to forged cheques. She had already spent two and a half years in Holloway and another sentence could herald the end for her.

I was beginning to see that being a useful witness was rather like mackeral fishing . . . you ran a number of lines from the boat and gave them a tug every now and then to see if anything was biting.

A while before I realised the necessity to return to London occasionally to retrace my steps and witness to the people who once knew me but I didn't expect spectacular results. Instead I would tug at the line occasionally, trusting God to do the rest. It was fascinating to see that the little tug to Anita was drawing her nearer to God.

About this time I also received news of Danny who had walked round the prison yard with me in Pentonville and whom I had later shared Christ with in Piccadilly. He had been abusive to me then; now I heard he was a Christian, great news.

Anita was still a registered addict so we had to make arrangements to pick up her prescriptions for drugs from the local surgery. She lived with us for a year or so and continued to collect her drugs and fix in the house, without making any moves towards becoming a Christian. It was a frustrating time and I needed all the patience the Holy Spirit could give me to prevent me from trying to force the issue. She slept with the light on, frightened of the dark, often imagining someone was trying to smother her. But she refused to turn to God for help. It was at this time that another old friend came to see us, Brian who had shared a room with me at Northwick Park. He had left Northwick to go back to his wife but was now back on drugs which saddened me. Like myself, Brian had a terrible past. Born in Holloway Prison where his mother was serving a sentence, he learnt to steal as a toddler. After leaving Life for the World he had done another term in prison. When freed he remarried a lovely girl called Helen, who herself had been in trouble and they had three boys.

He had just come out of mental hospital to find his wife had left him, and the children were living with Christian friends. Helen had had enough. Brian lived with us and after a while we invited Helen and the three children into the house as well.

In some ways inviting them to live with us was another of my mistakes, yet in the long run it worked out for them. I had miscalculated the pressures that come when two families live under the same roof. I still couldn't say 'no' to anyone needing practical or spiritual help.

We had become involved in a local community church and although it meant travelling some miles to the meetings had discovered fresh fellowship and spiritual encouragement. We were able to praise the Lord, dancing and raising our hands and worshipping in a really free fashion which I found refreshing after the more traditional churches I had been in contact with. At last, I thought, we had a spiritual home.

Things were improving. Despite the recurring friction at home it all seemed to be coming together.

Anita moved a mile or so away to live with a couple named Phil and Jenny who had recently come to live in the area with their three children. Phil was a scientist and had reached a point in his experiments when he decided there must be a God and challenged God to prove himself. He made a promise to God that he would go to Liverpool Cathedral and if the doors were open, he would go inside and give his life to God. And that's exactly what happened.

He met Commander Metters and had been found a home near us. The first night Phil came to see us he received the baptism in the Holy Spirit. We got to know them well, Phil's wife eventually became a Christian and joined us at the community church. Linda and Phil's wife were baptised in a local river on a beautiful spring evening.

They relieved us of our responsibilities towards Anita, still on drugs, so we had a little more freedom. But the friction between Brian and myself grew. I decided to move and let Brian and Helen have our home. I suspected him of all sorts of things and it was ruining our relationship. Linda and I found a little cottage set in a beautiful valley overlooking a stream, two miles from Hemyock: a miraculous discovery. The cottage had no bath, was damp and run-down, but we knew it was a gift from God. So we moved our bits and pieces from Twenty Acres and shifted to another period of our lives: a dark one.

A small offshoot of the community church we were attending started at Hemyock but things were not going too well. Linda was frank about a few problems with which the leadership seemed unable to help her.

We were tidying up the house one day when a telephone call came: Brian and Anita had been involved in a car crash and Anita had been arrested because drugs had been found in the car.

We also learned that the doctor's surgery had been broken into and drugs stolen. I felt instinctively that Brian was involved and that Anita was going to be the scapegoat. And when I discovered that Brian was on bail and Anita still in hospital and would only be released into police custody, my suspicions were even stronger. I jumped into the car and raced the fifty miles to see her in the hospital. Her story was very different. She told me Brian had broken into the surgery and turned up at her home later the same morning offering her a lift to London, and offering her the drugs she could have picked up legally later that day. She had agreed to go to London and help sell the drugs. Anita had acted stupidly and had made it worse by trying to cover up for Brian. I was able to convince her that it was for her own good and for Brian's in the long term that she should tell the truth. Reluctantly she agreed: made her statement, and when fit was released on bail.

I tried to tell the elders of the church what had happened but they insisted on taking Brian's side. I was already in conflict with them over the way Linda was being dealt with. Their teaching on covering, commitment and submission, good in themselves, seemed to fall down when it came to practicalities. I felt it was a retrograde step, back into my Roman Catholic past with its teaching of infallibility; one elder had told me to consider them correct, even if they were wrong! If I submitted, however, God would honour me.

The argument split open our fellowship with the leaders. One night Anita returned in tears after an elder had questioned her in a harsh manner. Linda went to see him, challenging him and his wife on the lack of sensitivity shown, but all that visit succeeded in achieving was a reprimand for my wife; a ban on attending the house group.

Bitterness and confusion twisted and tormented me. I often

think I have survived despite the church rather than because of it. Christians have little idea of how to deal with anyone with my past and didn't seem to want to learn either. Fortunately Christian friends rallied round and supported us, helping us through this time of bitterness. Much later a break came and we left the church since I refused to submit to any man, preferring to give Christ prior claim on my life.

Linda was depressed; the new house needed plenty of work; and the children had to be looked after. It was a desperate time for our family. Linda went to friends for a couple of days because she couldn't cope with the wrangling that was going on. She had suffered enough and I felt both of us were very close to mental breakdowns. But the Lord kept us.

I was clashing again with authority. With hindsight I realise there was much wrong in my attitudes; but also it needed Christian leaders with spiritual maturity to handle the situation and they weren't there.

As always, however, God touched us in our darkness in a miraculous way. Anita had come back to stay in our home after the accident and amazingly enough, as she listened to the arguments and discussions about the church, gave her heart to the Lord. It occurred late one evening. In the middle of an argument with an elder I suddenly felt we should pray for her. We talked into the early hours before she asked for prayer for forgiveness.

Brian was remanded in prison while waiting for the trial for his part in the surgery theft and his wife Helen was left on her own. I didn't know what to do, feeling awkward, but I couldn't see her left alone so I visited her from time to time. The church leaders had not been to see her and she needed help. Eventually, another miracle later, Brian was released, given a suspended sentence and re-united with Helen. It took time for our relationship to be healed but we were both honest and the rift was bridged.

So suddenly it seemed that things were beginning to go well at long last. The community church were very supportive of Anita and surrounded her with love and care after that one, careless interview, and gradually she began to come off drugs. She reduced her intake by one amp at a time; sometimes cutting half an amp, and over a year or so became completely free. She had much to come to terms with and needed deliverance and healing in her life but the work had begun. That was another miracle, one which unfolded over time.

During the months of bitter frustration with the church one event had taken place which had all the hallmarks of an isolated incident. Instead it became the first step in discovering what God had been training me for ever since I became a Christian, ten struggling years before.

I was to discover what God wanted from my life. And it all happened when I heard of a meeting in London . . .

16: A ministry is born

How kind of you to write, to spare the time to think of me and care. And thank you for the booklets they have been a great help. Meeting you and talking to you has made me question many aspects of my life and faith. Through reading and asking for help through prayer many things have taken on a new meaning.

L. Pucklechurch Remand Centre

I knew something special was going to happen as soon as I received the invitation to the inaugural meeting in London of the Prison Christian Fellowship. I had heard of Charles Colson, President Nixon's hatchet man who had been converted in prison after the Watergate Affair and launched a prison ministry in America. The opportunity to hear him speak was not to be missed. The meeting was at the headquarters of the Church of England, Church House, tucked away at the back of Westminster Abbey. There were many people there but it was an annoying affair for me. I heard Chuck Colson talk about the work in which he was involved and it sounded great; the possibility of transposing it across the Atlantic was exciting. Then Sylvia Mary Alison, wife of the Member of Parliament, Michael Alison, spoke of the need for such a work in Britain, talking in terms of a 'baby being born'. My expectations at the thought of it were shattered as I heard too many people talking about what they were doing and how they were trying to meet the need. It seemed any attempt to bring the many fragmented works to a unity in Christ was doomed.

I returned to Devon sad, but convinced that the work should begin, the baby be born. I was working like many others in various institutions, and opportunities were coming my way. But I was only one individual. There had to be a way of mobilising, training and encouraging others and Prison Christian Fellowship promised to be that way. We had to work as one, a complete united expression of God's love for prisoners.

I was so convinced about the need that I sat down as soon as I got home and wrote a letter to Sylvia Mary, trying to encourage her and pointing out that God was bigger than the frustrations of men. I told her she was suffering pre-natal depression. The fellowship would be born if she could bear the birth pangs. Little did I know the letter arrived when she was feeling low and wondering whether to continue with the move or not. As a direct result of that meeting another was arranged; this time a much more purposeful gathering. A prophecy was shared and Prison Christian Fellowship was obviously going to be formed in England.

It was to be an organisation that would bring me into contact with so many people who would have a tremendous influence on my life; with an organisation that would widen and develop the tentative ministry in which I had been engaged; and an organisation that would be a potentially mighty tool in God's hands.

As the fellowship moved through its birth pangs into life I was delighted to be part of a work that was such a challenge. At first I was given one hundred pounds a month and asked to look after the South-west region of Britain. My brief: to develop a growing liaison between chaplains and other prison officials and churches, drawing together the different strands of those working to change prisoners for Christ and those in churches who didn't even know what to pray for.

I was to form prayer groups to support individual institutions, spiritually and practically.

My first official meeting was to be in Exeter. I'd never organised anything like it before and really felt I was sailing uncharted waters. I decided to hold a morning meeting for a few key persons, a lunch-time get-together for a larger group of representatives: solicitors, ex-prisoners, probation officers, police officers, prison chaplains, people interested in praying, and church representatives. Then there would be an evening meeting open to the public.

Top of my list of invited guests was Percy Ashford, the

chaplain at Wandsworth Prison where I had first given my testimony as a young Christian years before. Rita Nightingale was to be the main speaker and Sylvia Mary joined us along with Ross Simpson, a senior probation officer from Harrow. I'd booked a massive church for the public meeting and waited with growing excitement. As it happened only a couple of rows in the whole church were filled. I was so disappointed, but the meeting had a touch of God about it. Rita spoke powerfully and I began to feel that great things were going to be achieved.

A group was born, significantly with the chaplain alongside whom I first stepped into prison work and who was later to become Chaplain General of the prison service.

My area ranged from Bournemouth to Bristol and to anywhere else in the west. It developed fast. That first meeting created a support group for Exeter Prison and within weeks another group had been formed in Weymouth until now there are twenty-one prayer groups, each one praying for institutions.

I set up lunchtime meetings and often the churches responded by putting on the lunches at their own expense. From these meetings a prayer group was usually formed to meet once a month.

I decided right from the start that the foundation of the work in my area would be prayer. Prayer, I was convinced, was like a bomber force going ahead to cut down the enemies' resistance as we waged a spiritual battle.

Linda's mother was the South-west area region co-ordinator for Lydia prayer groups which was a tremendous strength; their prayer was so helpful and they often helped practically, sometimes organising the lunches.

I had also come into contact with a couple who were to be major influences on the lives of Linda and myself, bringing balanced Christian truth hand-in-hand with practical help. While I was planning the Exeter meetings a lady telephoned me claiming that God was telling her to come to the morning get-together. I questioned her call, since that meeting was by invitation only and I was giving out the invitations! I was firm. There was no possibility of her coming.

Joyce phoned back later to reinforce her argument. At this point I began to have second thoughts. She was so adamant that

God had told her to be there, I didn't want to stand in God's way. I sent her an invitation. That particular meeting was chaotic. I had booked a small room in the Salt Cellar, a Christian coffee bar in Exeter, and the room was not big enough so we had to change venue at the last minute. Such was the unity among those present that it didn't seem to matter.

Joyce later introduced me to her husband, David Jubb, executive director of the London and Manchester Insurance Company – a wonderful Christian involved in the Full Gospel Businessmen's Fellowship. A friendship was born which was to last over the years.

I was beginning to see just how God was going to use the Prison Christian Fellowship. I could see the value of the Lydia prayer groups for focusing attention on to the need for prayer; I met with and appreciated the work of the Full Gospel Businessmen's Fellowship and could see that they were concentrating on their calling, reaching men for God through breakfasts and dinners; and now PCF was knitting together those involved in the work of ministry to those in prison, praying for and also ministering to staff and chaplaincy teams.

I suddenly realised that, as an ex-prisoner, I was mixing with probation officers, policemen, prison officers, governors, magistrates, chaplains, former prisoners and prisoners and yet we were all one in Christ.

My personal work at Portland Borstal now had a fresh urgency and because of the persistent and gentle guidance of Andrew I had become very acceptable. Even some of the non-Christian prison officers were co-operative, sensing that our efforts were for the benefit of the lads in their care.

There were those who didn't believe a prisoner could change, and felt I shouldn't be allowed to work in the institution. When I had a call to face the Governor my heart dropped, sensing that it was this view that was to be expressed. With weak knees I pushed open the door to his office and walked in. I stood nervously in front of him, not so much afraid as aware that it would take a miracle for me to be allowed to continue working at Portland. I relaxed as he smiled and motioned me to a chair. 'I've been thinking about your work here,' he started.

I was afraid he would hear the increased thumping of my

heart. 'I think you can do some good,' he continued to my astonishment and referred to a move to make me a catechist (an official assistant to the chaplain) which would enable me to have an official Home Office pass and give me the opportunity to enter Borstal on a regular basis. He probed and questioned me for a few minutes and then agreed to support the application. He assured me of his support for my work. 'If you have any trouble – get in touch with me,' he invited.

I was over the moon. A catechist at the borstal where I had done my time. That was really something. Yet another thread had been woven into the work God was encouraging me to do.

But at home things were heading towards a torrid conclusion. I had stopped going to the fellowship since Linda had been barred from the house group meetings. Many of our Christian friends had stopped visiting her because they were still linked with the fellowship and had been told she was a disturbing influence. This hurt me deeply. I knew the practical love she had shown to so many who had passed through our home. So when I was away for a few days, as often happened, it meant that Linda shouldered the burdens of the home alone. She was totally isolated, except for a few friends who ignored the church instructions.

God was pushing me on with fresh hopes for my prison work. I knew it was right and yet I recognised things could not carry on in the home like this for long. I knew Satan would attack the home base and for a while didn't know how to juggle the two pressures.

The two ends of the equation started to tug in different directions, they stretched and strained and I felt myself being torn. How could I decide on my future?

I leaned heavily on David and Joyce. God had provided them in a miraculous way and they recognised the needs that Linda and I had and stepped in to help. God always seemed to bring someone across our paths at the right time.

As they helped at home my work with the PCF began to expand as I discovered many people with the same commitment to prisoners. More and more opportunities came to enter prisons and talk about my faith and teach from the Bible. I was discovering that if I entered quietly and kept firmly to the time limits allowed I could do everything God wanted me to do.

Each prison, of course, had its own system. Some refused to allow me to enter, even those with quite low security ratings, and others, including some highly rated prisons, let me in. It was entirely the decision of the governors, chaplains or the Prison Officers' Association or security officers. We were dealing with men, but God kept opening doors; sometimes so many that I had difficulties keeping up with them.

I became Southern co-ordinator of the fellowship, a much wider region with contacts in many more prisons, institutions and groups involved in the work. I realised that on my own I could only do so much; mobilising others would release them to do important work. So I met Christians from a variety of denominations and began to see things move.

Because of Linda's isolated situation and the treatment of the church we decided to move back to the Sidmouth area, at least Linda's family were there and Fred and Wendy. David and Joyce were nearby too.

We had no money and no possibilities of a mortgage but Linda and I and the children were invited into the home of a couple who, although not regular churchgoers, showed us a lot of love and kindness. I discovered later that Maureen, the wife was involved with the Jehovah's Witnesses. Since then Fred and Wendy have helped lead her to Jesus.

It was not long before we were able to rent a place of our own, another miracle. It was a cottage in Newton Poppleford, where Linda had once lived. It jutted almost into the main road through the town, a small home with three bedrooms and a bathroom upstairs; two rooms and a kitchen downstairs. It was like heaven to the whole family. Things were now falling into place. It seemed that as soon as we left the Hemyock area a huge load had been lifted from my shoulders.

Anita had been growing in the Lord and was now living in a caravan near the fellowship, getting her life together. I was being paid part-time for my work with Prison Fellowship and other Christians often sent gifts which were a great help.

The desert was behind us. As Linda and I carried the last pieces of furniture into the new home we sensed the burden being lifted from us.

I was facing up to the challenges of my marriage. A friend spoke firmly to me one day about whether or not I was ministering to my family's needs properly. I was now working at it.

Linda spent a week-end with friends in St Ives and was delighted with the warm welcome she received at the Anglican church in Halsetown. The minister, Father John Harper, was encouraging and Linda was accepted for who she was. I had been brought into contact with that church through a borstal lad who had gone back to that area. I had previously visited the church myself and preached. Love and warmth, commodities we had missed for so long, flowed over me. And just as God was touching our private lives He was leaning heavily on my work in prisons also.

Through the work and our relationship with Sylvia Mary, Linda and I were invited to the House of Commons to celebrate the silver anniversary of Michael and Sylvia's marriage. As chairman of PCF Sylvia was holding a tea-party at the House. The prospect of tea in Parliament was something that pleased Linda and I so we set off from Devon with great excitement . . . until the car broke down about half-way. I was all for giving up but Linda had the bit between her teeth and suggested we thumb a lift. So we stood at the side of the road with our suitcase waving a thumb at the traffic. God was ready again, this time in the shape of a young man who drove us to the outskirts of London and listened patiently as I gave him my testimony.

We jumped on a train with little time to spare, but realising we also needed to change for our appointment. As the train pulled into a station we did a double change – slipped into the toilets to reappear in our best clothes, and changed platforms for Westminster, after depositing our cases in the left luggage department.

We arrived at Westminster fifteen minutes late. But even in the rush through the labyrinth that was the Houses of Parliament I couldn't fail to praise God for the dramatic change He had made to lead me to this experience.

Looking over the Thames I reflected on the years before when I had been sleeping rough on the opposite bank. What a transformation!

Prison Fellowship had actually started in Parliament as

my old friend John Harris and a number of Members of Parliament, with Sylvia Mary, had met to pray about such a ministry. That was a couple of years before the first inaugural meeting. Linda and I recognised many faces at the tea-party who had merely been names before . . . the Prime Minister, leading members of Parliament.

Unfortunately I made one mistake. What I took to be fruit juice turned out to be a potent champagne cocktail and because I rarely drank it wasn't long before I felt myself becoming a little woozy. I regretted letting my guard down, feeling there were opportunities to witness during that afternoon. Perhaps, however, God had other plans.

Linda and I eventually left, picking up our luggage from the station and made our way to the home of a girl who had become a Christian at the coffee bar in Sidmouth many years before. We met her husband and stayed the night enjoying their Christian company.

It was a day of contrasting circumstances: hitching a lift to London; a party in Parliament; and meeting an old friend. Life was like that now – packed with variety and challenge. I certainly knew what John 10:10 meant when Jesus said he came to give life more abundantly.

I was speaking at Erlstoke Youth Custody Centre with Peter Saunt and we called the lads forward for prayer. Rarely did many lads come forward, it needed too much courage to do so in front of their friends. On this occasion a dozen youngsters came to the front and we laid hands on them and prayed.

Part of the frustration in preaching in prison so often is that I realise that as soon as the service is over the men have to go back to their cells and it is not possible to talk much to those who have come forward. Still, God knows them and is able to work through the Holy Spirit unrestricted by prison bars or walls.

I did a Bible study on one occasion for a group of sixteen or eighteen lads and a prison officer had to sit in as the chaplain was involved in other things. I was speaking on suffering and pointed out that the life of a Christian is not always easy. Afterwards the officer spoke to me. He had lost his faith when his child had died. We were able to pray and talk about God's love.

Even chaplains are sometimes helped. They are under tremendous pressure with so many needs around them. I cannot forget the day I was talking to a chaplain when he began to question me about the baptism in the Holy Spirit. Suddenly he knelt and asked me to pray for him. Linda was with me at the time and we prayed and laid hands on him, despite feeling a little awkward.

It is tremendous when I discover the chaplain is keen to minister to the men, sometimes the chaplains don't know Christ personally and I have met prisoners who have been put off Christianity because of the chaplain's attitude and lack of conviction.

Occasionally my journeys have brought me into contact with others outside the prison. And I have been helped by them, even non-Christians. The first time I was invited to preach in Parkhurst Prison on the Isle of Wight was one such occasion.

It was a busy day. I had spoken in the prison and had fellowship with the chaplain and also spent some time with my Prison Christian Fellowship colleague John Stewart, the county's evangelist. I'd visited Jason, a Christian prisoner seeking to be a witness to his fellow inmates.

I had been given a lift to the ferry ready to return to Portsmouth. I noticed a man waiting by the ferry who had been in the waiting room at prison earlier. He was a burly, hard-looking fellow from London. He told me he took time off work every six weeks or so to visit his brother. The East-ender wasn't a Christian and told me how difficult it was to find different things to talk about on the visits, especially after the first hour in the visiting room. He had been visiting his brother for six years.

Then he looked at me and said, 'But of course I have to do it, he's my brother, isn't he?'

His words struck me with real force. That's what the Prison Christian Fellowship is all about: a commitment to visit, and seek to support, brothers and sisters in the prisons.

Those words have never left me. They have, in fact, become part of my ministry ideal: each time I visit a prison I recall them; I'm visiting my brothers and sisters.

17: Travelling man

When I left Dorchester and returned here I immediately applied for a transfer back to the South-west region but was refused by the Home Office. As you know that is final. After a few weeks I thought, why not ask God Himself if He could do anything? So I got on my knees and prayed and what do you think happened? I only got my security rating reduced so now I am eligible for a semi-open prison. Now they say they have been told to move me to Dartmoor as soon as possible. Then I applied for a correspondence course in agriculture which was refused because the HO said it was too expensive. Again I prayed. The education officer came to see me just before dinner today and said the course had been approved.

M. Hull Prison.

As I journey around for PCF, visiting prisons and youth custody centres, I am amazed what God can do through me as I continually surrender my life to Him. Because of my record and the deep problems I have faced in my life I am constantly reminded of how weak I am. Every time I visit a prison or see a drug addict I feel a surge of emotion, recalling what God has rescued me from. And yet Christ uses a weak instrument such as myself . . . My visits make me more aware than ever that I don't know all the answers, but I care. I have a love for the chaplains who want to serve Christ and reach men for Him. On one trip recently I was invited to speak at a youth rally in Scunthorpe, outside my normal area and the first time I had been north on prison business. As I drove to the first meeting which was to be with a PCF group in Hull I picked up a dishevelled man standing by the side of the road. I was only five or six miles from the end of my journey but our short conversation was enough to establish that the man who had helped me at the start of my pilgrimage, Norman Ingram-Smith, was still working faithfully at St Martins-in-the-Fields, London. Norman had given this man a fiver and put him on the road that morning. The man had been in prison and, unable to cope since being released, was on his way north to have a break from London. I shared what God had done for me and as I reached across to open the door to let him out I rejoiced in the goodness of God. Only that morning he had been with Norman and now, a couple of hundred miles north, a full circle had been formed.

After the meeting in Hull I spent the evening with a lovely couple who are burdened for prisoners and visit men in Hull prison and are becoming positively involved with prisoners there. I also found they were writing to a prisoner whom I had been in contact with in Dartmoor, a very violent criminal named Malcolm.

Malcolm had been involved in a police hostage drama. The only reason he was alive was because a police marksman's radio had broken down. Over a period of eighteen months the couple had quietly given him support and eventually he came to know Christ. This illustrates perfectly the faithfulness of those who support prisoners, write to them, or offer hospitality.

The next day I moved on to visit Ivor Halliwell who had been chaplain at Exeter and was now working in Wakefield Prison. Another hitch-hiker stopped me on the journey. He claimed that the church was full of hypocrisy and he resented anything Christian. As we talked, however, he began to listen and I prayed with him when I stopped the car at his destination.

Arriving in Wakefield I realised I had no idea where the prison was. I pulled into the side of the road and asked directions from a woman with a young child waiting at a bus stop. They were travelling in the same direction as myself so I gave them a lift. Apparently the child was hyperactive and they were going to a hospital. Again I was able to talk about what God had done for me and plant more gospel seeds. After giving them a copy of my LP record I dropped them off.

At the prison Ivor met me and we went out for lunch and

relaxed together. It was good to talk and share Jesus and feel a spirit of assurance and concern knowing we were one in Christ.

Ivor then took me to see a prisoner I had known in Exeter. The man had made a commitment but had problems holding his Christian life together. He was doing a life sentence and was on rule 43; he was isolated a lot. I recalled the name but didn't remember the man until I entered the visiting room. A time of darkness had overcome him and despite his faith voices had been speaking in his head and he felt he was cracking up. He was aware of slipping away from God but had been unable to help himself, and had ceased going to church.

I realised just how easy it was for Christians outside prison; given a problem, they invariably have someone to turn to or a friend to comfort them. This man had no-one. When he suffered he was alone in his cell, except for his life-line, the chaplaincy team and visits from lay-people. We prayed and I felt Christ reach out to him. It is hard for prisoners to keep a commitment to the Lord – one of the reasons so many fall away on discharge.

After the visit I had an hour to spare and, needing a haircut, decided to try a local barber. I ignored two barbers' shops, I don't know why, and went into the third. The barber was a man in his late fifties and began to talk, as all barbers seem to. It wasn't long before I told him the reason I was in Wakefield and he was saying, 'Praise the Lord, brother.' I had entered the shop of a Pentecostal man with a deep peace in his heart and joy on his face.

For twenty minutes we shared experiences, I had my hair cut and my faith uplifted as I learned of the many people he had prayed with in that chair.

On the road out of Wakefield I was aiming for Scunthorpe and the youth rally and a young couple of hitch-hikers sat and listened to my testimony.

In Scunthorpe I arrived at the home of a couple who were to put me up for the night: he was a lively Christian, full of humour and warm-hearted. I also met Eric Smart, the PCF leader in Scunthorpe and we talked about the meeting to be held that evening. What thrilled me particularly about those people was that they lived sixty miles from the nearest prison and yet they were deeply involved in following up men and women from their area who had been in trouble. This humbled me; the amount of work done by lay people around the country is amazing, and yet they are few in number.

At the youth meeting there was a smattering of older people plus a few former prisoners and a prisoner's wife. Many of those had been reached through a work in a transport cafe which the church ran in the centre of the town. Eric told me they were also considering opening a house to help those from prison. This was significant as the main problem for prisoners on their release is the lack of a home. Without it they almost invariably return to prison.

As I journeyed back to Devon after those few busy but normal days I reflected on the people I had met and been with . . . ordinary people with a burden for those in trouble and a willingness to reach out and do something practical as well as pray. Names come to me . . . Jill, Jan and Joyce . . . Geoff . . . Peter . . . Vernon . . . people from all denominations. Our work behind prison walls takes away the denominational labels that sometimes blind us with prejudice. I find it exhilarating to work with the whole body of Christ for a common cause.

I rejoiced because I knew that in Wakefield Prison, with seven hundred men trapped for life, there is a group of prisoners who meet, pray, study the Bible, and worship God. Many prisons have similar groups.

God is moving as Christians pray and work together, but we are still only scratching the surface. There is so much to do and the church is slowly learning to respond to the needs in our prisons.

18: International flavour

I am a condemned prisoner here at Maximum Security Prison for eight years. I received Jesus Christ as my personal Saviour and Lord in prison in 1977. Praise the Lord for your much appreciated love towards me and my friends. We enjoyed spiritual food in prayer meetings, Bible studies, church services and many good things although we are in Death Row.

B. Maximum Security Prison, Kabwe, Zambia

I was invited to Ireland for an international conference with the Northern Ireland Prison Fellowship. I had been getting news of the international work of Prison Christian Fellowship for some time but this was to be an opportunity to see and hear of that work first-hand, and also to renew the acquaintance of Chuck Colson whose inspiration had fired me at the launch of our own prison work two years before.

I met Darrell Hayes, who had served a life sentence for murder and is now training director for PF International in Canada . . . a man who had previously been merely a name on a prayer letter. A brother from Sri Lanka was at the conference; he had sold his stove to buy the air ticket to the conference. A worker from Peru, a member of the Full Gospel Businessmen's Fellowship International told me of his work in Lima Prison where thousands of inmates are herded together, men and women and where the children belonging to the women are growing up in prison. Some of the youngsters are twelve years old and have never been outside the prison. He told me of the punishments inflicted on prisoners, some placed in boxes so small they cannot stand.

It opened my eyes to the world-wide work of organisations such as ours.

Since that conference I have received prayer letters from abroad with a new vision: anxious to pray for others and support them in that vital way.

I received a letter recently from a prisoner in Zambia in a condemned cell, pleading for literature and prayer for himself and other brothers in Christ in that prison. He is probably dead by now, but I'm confident we'll meet in heaven.

When I now see Papua New Guinea on the map I know there are committed people there reaching those in prison.

Australia, New Zealand and Canada – all have men and women sacrificially giving time and money to extend God's kingdom behind bars.

I was also challenged by the commitment of people from the Third World who made supreme efforts to be with us in Ireland.

I consider the western world, America, Europe and particularly Britain, where many of the offenders are from a background similar to my own; thrown from home to home, often with no-one to care, orphans, abandoned, slipping and slithering into a world of drugs and crime, and I know that God is not only concerned with holiness and righteousness – but also justice.

Our prisons are overcrowded and there are many things which ought to be changed but we don't have the torture and starvation many prisoners find in their life in institutions abroad. Our system destroys the will of a man in a very subtle way, leaving him institutionalised and stripped of human dignity.

In Ireland I was moved by the power of God to change lives. I stood next to a former IRA lad who had done fifty-five days hunger strike and a man who was a former UDA prisoner. We worshipped together: one in Christ. An ex-Marxist guerilla, active against the Government on the Phillipines, was there; he had bombed and machine-gunned so-called enemies – now he was with us in our world-wide work, a Christian working alongside a Christian General who was at one time his sworn enemy. All these men work under the threat of death, their former friends now enemies.

My experience in Northern Ireland was to have a profound effect on my life as I realised I was not just part of the body of Christ in Britain, but a vast, world-wide ministry. Since that conference I've not read a newspaper without having to pray for a trouble spot in the world which I know has prisoners and people working for them. As someone said, 'I can't do everything for everyone; but I can do something for someone.' I want to do that something and to share in the work of Prison Christian Fellowship doing it.

There are practical things apart from prayer. One of the men I met in Ireland lives in South Africa and runs a community where men and women, many from prison backgrounds, work on a farm project. It provides employment and a home. He's a man of vision and imagination doing what he can for those he can, one of so many used by the Holy Spirit to meet the many needs of those caught up in the penal systems of the world.

19: Full circle

I've felt so alone in life but with you and Anita coming into my life I feel I am not alone. I'm so thankful I've been praying and my prayers are being answered. The staff here have realised I have found Christianity and have put my life and faith in Jesus Christ. They are pleased for the way I'm trying so hard to change my life.

J. St Lawrence's Hospital, Bodmin

The dark tunnel was behind me. All of a sudden I began to realise that God had taken Linda, myself, Abigail and Naomi through a long, dark experience, sometimes through my own foolishness, and I was stepping out into glorious light. I was enjoying my children; life was fun as well as hard work; my whole family life was stable and free from many of the pressures which had created instant trouble spots in the past.

I'd spent a life-time escaping; from the army, from borstal, from prisons; from drugs and from myself and my past. Now, at last, I'd escaped to reality. I had something real in my life, and all because of the miraculous power of Christ. Of one thing I was certain: I wouldn't be escaping again, there was nothing to escape from.

It was as if dark clouds had slowly but certainly blown away and the sun was shining. We had lived in our rented cottage for quite a while when the opportunity came to set up a trust and buy the property. I had had the vision of a trust which David and Joyce and others took to heart, put flesh on the bones, and set up Stepping Stones Fellowship Trust, based in Devon, to support our work.

Through the Trust we are moving towards getting a house for young offenders and, in time, somewhere for women in trouble. This is the long-term vision.

Prison Christian Fellowship is also moving on. Other co-ordinators have been appointed in various parts of the country and we meet regularly to pray and discuss mutual problems which is a tremendous help. Obviously as with any new work there have been times of tension and heart-ache. Rev Peter Timms was appointed chairman and new ideas were instituted. Not all of us felt they were right. Ross Simpson and John Harris have gone, and yet as we meet in the national leadership group there is an ex-policeman, an ex-governor, a Home Office inspector, a probation officer, an ex-business-man and two ex-prisoners. In human terms we shouldn't be able to relate, but in Christ we do, however not without some struggles!

Tom Marriott has been running a house in West Malling (St Benedicts, part of an Anglican closed order of nuns who pray for our work), as a training centre for PCF, a place for retreats where hundreds drift through, ex-prisoners, chaplains, governors, prison officers and lay people involved in support work. Tom moved there with his wife Doris and their family and it has become a place of peace and refreshment.

More and more I am writing letters to prisoners and former prisoners, and invitations to go to prisons are increasing. My work in Portland continues, though borstals have now become Youth Custody Centres. Martin Kiddle is the new chaplain. I meet regularly with him and his wife Megs, working for the Lord. I have often been on trips with Rita Nightingale, and her enthusiasm and testimony is a constant encouragement.

On one journey I was to speak in two churches with Rita. At the first I wondered why I was there; the attendance was very sparse and the people enjoyed Rita's testimony of how she had been in prison in Thailand facing a twenty year sentence when she found Christ and was miraculously released. I spoke of the work of PCF but it didn't seem I was needed.

In the second meeting, much better attended, I was well into my talk when I noticed Peter and Pru Coad. Peter is a senior probation officer in Bristol and PCF leader for the area. They had a dark-haired, young attractive girl with them. Afterwards Peter explained she had just left a rehabilitation centre in Hampshire. When I spoke to her I realised she was stoned, under the influence of drugs. Peter had found her and booked her into a local guest house for two or three nights.

I led Carol out of the church, away from the chattering crowd, and we sat on the church steps. Almost without invitation she began to talk. 'I've been to prison. I've been a prostitute and done terrible things. I don't think God would want me.' I assured her God did care and was interested. Because she was so drugged it was pointless talking much that evening so I arranged to see her at the guest house the following day.

Next day Carol remembered little of our conversation of the previous evening but was open and willing to talk. At twenty-seven she had four children – all in care and, amazingly enough, all with the same Christian couple. Carol had been involved in the drug scene in Amsterdam and had quite a name in her home town, Bristol. At different stages she had lived with men and been briefly involved in prostitution having a string of broken relationships behind her. At the Christian rehabilitation centre she had made a commitment of sorts but was vulnerable and had slipped back into drugs. Carol felt tremendously guilty about the children and had been badly hurt over the years, including having a father who had been violent towards her mother.

I realised we needed to pray and lay many of her troubles and burdens at the feet of Jesus Christ. I also knew it was unwise to minister to Carol on my own so I took her to Peter's house and we asked Pru to pray with us. I felt it necessary to pray for Carol to be baptised in the Spirit so that she had power over both drugs and her lifestyle. We prayed. Carol began to weep: God was using her tears to wash away the past. Pru and I cuddled her and comforted her. I'm sure it helped to know she was accepted, our arms represented the arms of Jesus.

I believe Carol needed an operation with the Holy Spirit as a surgeon. Just as a tumour or cancer can't be seen, but is felt by the sufferer, so those with deep-rooted spiritual cancers need the Holy Spirit to remove them to set them free.

At the bottom of our garden is a small tree, for years wrapped with an ever tightening ivy-plant. I could have tried to pull away the leaves, but the best way to free the tree was to attack the ivy at its roots. It all died away.

I've discovered on a number of occasions when dealing with people who have surface problems such as drugs or drink that the real deadly issues are often deep inside where only the Holy Spirit can reach.

Because the centre wouldn't take Carol back (she had been disruptive) she came to stay at our house, sleeping on the floor in one of the two small rooms downstairs. She was free from much of the past but over the weeks it became apparent that something was still stifling her new life. As we discussed her history I found she had been actively involved in the occult over the years. Anita and myself prayed with Carol one evening: a long night of struggling. Although at one stage I felt we had taken on too much our prayers, finally broke through and we felt the chains snapping. I believe that night Carol was set free from unclean spirits and also the past influences which were the roots of her sexual and family problems.

Carol lived for a time in a caravan next to our house and grew stronger all the time. She helped me with secretarial work and cared for guests who visited us. She is now working as a waitress in a local hotel, living in and beginning to find her own feet. Carol's transformation is a miracle. She has, in fact, ministered with me to others in her former situation, bringing the message of the changing power of the Bible to life. Anita has also been with me to various institutions giving her story. In Pucklechurch Remand Centre recently she gave her story to an audience which included the governor of the borstal where she was many years ago.

As our lives were coming together at Newton Poppleford and the prison ministry expanding, I still retained a niggling feeling that we ought to be doing something locally: something nearer our home. I didn't want our house to be merely a place from which I moved all over the country.

Wandering into Sidmouth one day I had an urge to look up the old coffee bar, The Haven. It was still there, tucked away in its little side street. But now it was deserted, the furniture in an untidy heap, the rooms unused. The church had given up the coffee bar and other local organisations decided not to use it so it had been returned to the YMCA. My mind began to move. Was this what God had for the future?

I contacted local YMCA officials and to my amazement they told me the previous month a decision to sell the building should have been made by the southern region committee. For various reasons the plan was shelved. Yet again I had that feeling that the Holy Spirit was planning ahead of me.

I met Tony Miles, the local YMCA representative, and told him of my dream: to re-open the coffee bar as a centre for ministry. He was interested and introduced me to members of the region at their next meeting. Approval was given for me to re-open The Haven under the auspices of the YMCA. So I was back in the building which God had used when I began my work for him.

I was a bit apprehensive about working with the YMCA until I learned from Tony and John Naylor, the national secretary, that not only did they love God but there was a move to bring the organisation back to its original Christian foundations. I also came into contact with Stephen Hayles, the minister at Emmanuel church and we were reconciled, a marvellous occasion. He is now on the council of reference for the coffee bar.

The building needed a lot of redecoration: Anita and Carol are helping to lick it into shape.

The drugs problem is chronic in Devon, as in many parts of the country, and there is a desperate need for personnel to reach out to those crushed and enslaved by addiction.

I'm working in my office, the back room of The Haven, smelling the fresh new paint. Around me is the sound of work. John is ripping up floorboards ready to lay new joists; Julian is drilling holes in the walls as we prepare to rewire the building; and Anita and Carol are rearranging the furniture.

We've already received gifts of £3,600 towards the extensive building work from anonymous donors, and Susy, one of the helpers, had her broken foot miraculously healed as we prayed. God is blessing us.

There is a lot of work ahead and I can't lessen my activities in relation to prisons and youth custody centres, they are too important. But God has given me a fresh challenge back in the area where I was a borstal boy.

In a few months the coffee bar will be humming again, although I trust I shan't be making some of the mistakes I made in the past. I've got lots of ideas for local and national ministries but I want God to lead. I'm prepared to take it slowly; and I will try not to let down my family.

But I feel something is going to happen here, and God hasn't failed yet.

20: Hello, mum

The Lord is great indeed to have blessed me with your visit. Apart from meeting each other in the flesh you were able to encourage and answer for me many questions. Praise him loudly.

J. Parkhurst Prison

When I got married the question of my background came up. In fact I had tried to develop a relationship again with my adopted parents over the years but found if difficult; I had hurt them a lot and my mother, a fervent Roman Catholic, felt that my conversion was unreal. In her eyes I had always been a Christian because I had been baptised and confirmed as a child.

It was always a strained relationship. I suppose, on reflection, I had only spent a few years of my life with them. I had, in fact, been longer in prison and other institutions than with them over the years. My life of crime and drugs had hurt them deeply.

I didn't blame them for questioning whether anyone like me could change overnight. It was, after all, a miracle.

I always knew I had a real mother and that I had been born illegitimately. It hadn't affected me deeply and I had no real desire to discover my mother again after all those years, though now and then I considered it. Once the children were born, however, Linda began to think about my real mother. Perhaps mother would like to see her grandchildren, she suggested. With that gentle encouragement I began the search.

By then the law had changed and adopted children were allowed access to some social services records to discover their original parents. I started to take the first steps but it seemed an age before anything happened, although it did give me the opportunity to share Christ with a social worker.

I had an interview with the local social services and they assessed my reason for wanting to find my mother. Eventually they made documents available to me giving my childhood history. It made a fascinating story.

The first thing that hit me was that though I had always believed I had been adopted once, by the Ralls, now I untangled the threads to discover I had been adopted twice: my real name was Albert John Dansie. One name more than I thought I had. I had been born to Lilian May Dansie towards the end of the war, at a time when there was little social help and my mother had been living with her mother and stepfather. Pressure had been put upon her to have me adopted, the alternative being that she would have to go to what was known as the poor house. She allowed a couple living in the house with the family at the time, the Durstons, to look after me. They were an older couple and mother gave them money when she could afford to.

They moved away with me eventually, having adopted me, and, through a lodger, mother discovered that the conditions under which I was living were not suitable. She reported the Durstons to the authorities. They were arrested and imprisoned for neglect and I went to a home.

My mother then married again and made vain efforts to get me back. Social services officials would not allow it. I was put in an orphanage and eventually the Ralls adopted me, my second adoption and third change of name. They were not fully briefed about my past and had really wanted a girl but were persuaded to take me instead.

As I read all this it was like reading an adventure story about someone else. It seemed unreal.

I arranged to see a social worker in Plymouth and was given additional information plus court records. For two years I did nothing: should I dig into the past any more?

I was given the name of my mother but couldn't bring myself to do anything else. Eventually I found myself in Plymouth with PCF group leader David Knott. He discovered what I knew and took me to the local library where we used the electors' roll and traced two married women with the name Lilian May Young and Lily May Young, a tedious task. I wrote down the addresses but still took it no further.

Finally Linda persuaded me to go to Plymouth to try and find my mother. I was apprehensive and my worries were eased when the car developed a leaky petrol tank. Linda wasn't to be put off. Her father agreed to take us and they dropped me off on the seafront with the girls while they checked the addresses. I spent the afternoon with the children climbing rocks and playing on the beach. It seemed like hours later that Linda's father appeared. His face showed they had been successful. They had found my mother.

Linda had rung the bell at the council house in the suburbs of Plymouth. A short, dark-haired woman answered the door. Linda asked, 'Are you Mrs Young?'

Linda was carrying a file with all my details in and the woman, glanced at the file, and expected a social worker. 'It isn't trouble is it?' she asked, worried about her son.

Linda continued: 'I have some information which may be of interest to you . . . ' she paused, 'concerning Albert John.'

Linda didn't know whether it was the right Mrs Young. It was. Mother's eyes filled with tears. 'After all these years,' she wept. They wept together. Linda stayed while her father came for me.

I climbed into the car and we drove to the house. I didn't know what to do. I nervously walked up the short path and rang the doorbell. Mother answered.

She looked ten years younger than I imagined her to be. I hugged her, 'Hello mum,' I said. She was weeping and I kept my arms round her praying and praising God.

I often wondered what would happen if I ever met my real mother, now I knew. The children met their new grandmother, another emotional meeting.

She was sixty-five and felt very guilty about what had happened all those years ago; I suppose she had never forgiven herself. I made it clear that I forgave her.

We stayed about an hour and made arrangements to return and spend a weekend with her later. Neither of us can make up for the lost years, thirty years had gone by since the tiny boy of five had been taken to the orphanage and adopted again.

Mother's husband had died ten years before our meeting. They had two children a boy, ironically named Tony, and a girl,

Maureen. I met them both over the following few months.

Our growing friendship was celebrated last Christmas: my mother never forgot that I had been born on Christmas Eve and still had a photograph of me when a child. Each year at Christmas she had shed tears for the boy she had lost. Last Christmas was a true family occasion with Linda, Abigail, Naomi, me, Mum, Tony and Maureen. It was a wonderful time . . . God had already begun to make up for the lost years.

I've never blamed mother for any of what happened. After all, I was strong-willed and followed the wrong course of my own free will. But meeting her has given me one more thing to pray for: I long for mother and my newly discovered half-brother and sister to know the same Saviour I have found.

God has restored my relationship with Him; brought me back to my family; now I long for them to discover His love. After all, if it wasn't for the changing power of Jesus Christ I would either be dead (another statistic killed by drugs) or still wasting my life in Prison.

So much has happened yet there is so much potential still. 'If anyone is in Christ he is a new creature' (2 Corinthians 5:17). Jesus has delivered me from the past and given me a future. And He is restoring the 'years the locusts have eaten,' as He promised He would. Where men had given up God took over and proved that miracles are not a thing of the past.

If you would like details of the work of Prison Fellowship please write to:

Prison Fellowship (England and Wales),
P.O. Box 945,
Chelmsford,
Essex CM2 7PX

Tony Ralls can also be contacted through this address.

'A bruised reed he will not break, and a smouldering wick he will not snuff out.' Isaiah 42:3

Also available on Social Needs by M. Tony Ralls
Suitable for outreach and education for Christians

Literature

Snatched from the Flames – the story of a woman who against all the odds overcame abuse and violence as a child and seventeen years of drug addiction. (With Anita Hydes) New Wine Press/Marshalls £1.95

What everyone should know about drugs – a must for those wishing to be informed. New Wine Press £1.00

The Bitter Harvest – an up to date look at current social problems with practical insights and guidelines on how to help. New Wine Press £2.50

Out of His Darkness – 14 page comic on the life of Tony Ralls

Music

Life LP – songs by M. Tony Ralls.
Produced by the Daylight Co. Cassette/LP £3.50

Bitter Harvest cassette – songs based on the same theme. Produced by the Daylight Co./New Wine Press £4.95 (cassette only)

Videos (mission Recordings/Tony Ralls)

Out of darkness – half hour documentary on M. Tony Ralls and family with 5 short discussion starters.

The Writing on the Wall – Drugs education video suitable for preventative education for young people. Filmed at Portland Youth Custody Centre. Price £20.00

Snatched from the Flames – Anita Hydes' story and ministry £20.

Who cares? – 6 lads from Care Backgrounds speak out. Filmed at Portland Youth Custody Centre £20.

Teaching cassettes

Christian response to Social Issues (double cassette)
Three sides teaching, fourth testimony £2.00

History of Drugs - practical insights £2.00

Books and Bitter Harvest cassette available through Christian bookshops or by post from:

Y.M.C.A., Mill Street,
Sidmouth,
Devon,
England

Other items from YMCA only. Proceeds channeled back into areas of social need.

For regular prayer/information sheet on the ministry of Tony Ralls write to:

Stepping Stones Trust
20 Wendover Way,
Exeter,
Devon EX2 6JG
England

'I was in prison and you visited me' Matthew 25:36